Going Everywhere with Jesus

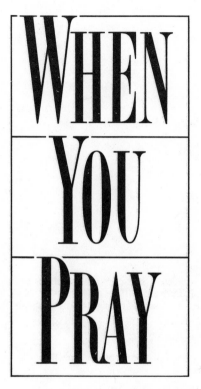

WHEN YOU PRAY

Going Everywhere with Jesus

E. DEE FREEBORN

Foreword by Steve Harper

BEACON HILL PRESS OF KANSAS CITY
KANSAS CITY, MISSOURI

Unless otherwise indicated, all Scripture quotations are from *The Holy Bible, New International Version* (NIV), copyright 1973, 1978, 1984 by the International Bible Society. Used by permission of Zondervan Bible Publishers.

Permission to quote from other copyrighted versions of the Bible is acknowledged with appreciation:

The *Amplified Bible* (Amp.). The *Amplified New Testament*, © 1958 by the Lockman Foundation.

The *New English Bible* (NEB), © The Delegates of the Oxford University Press and The Syndics of the Cambridge University Press, 1961, 1970.

The New Testament in the Language of the People (Williams), by Charles B. Williams. Copyright 1937 by Bruce Humphries, Inc.; assigned 1949 to Moody Bible Institute, Chicago.

King James Version (KJV).

10   9   8   7   6   5   4   3   2   1

To my mother, Helen Jean Freeborn,
who taught me at an early age
the value of prayer.

Contents

Foreword

I may never forget Dee Freeborn's definition of prayer, one he gleaned from observing his mother-in-law: going everywhere with Jesus. You will never forget a lot of what you are about to read in this inspiring book.

Prayer is one of those things in the Christian life that is always one generation away from extinction. Consequently, we never exhaust the need for new books on the subject. But we need books that, while fresh, are rooted in Scripture and the rich insights of church history. This is such a book.

Prayer is one of those things we never fully master. Consequently, we are always in Christ's school of prayer, being reminded of things we must not forget and being introduced to things we must not omit from a developing life of prayer. We need books that keep us mindful of what we already know and help us to be watchful for what we need to know. This is a book like that.

Finally, prayer is a spiritual art. Every artist knows that one learns best little by little, adding nuance after nuance to the basic design. So, we need books that lead us along, step by step, rather than overwhelming us all at once. This book does that.

Perhaps most of all, we need to know that we are made for prayer. True prayer arises from a heart created to pray. It is a hunger more than a duty. It is an invitation more than an obligation. It is a fulfillment more than a formula.

The saints have not prayed because they had to so much as they prayed because they wanted to. Prayer is the expression of deepest desire, it is the lifting of the mind and heart to God for honest dialogue and intimate communion. I hope this book will enrich your ability to do that, and to know indeed that God is "only a prayer away."

—STEVE HARPER, PH.D.
Professor of Spiritual Formation
Asbury Theological Seminary

Acknowledgments

So many good people have a hand in the completion of a project such as this one. I am grateful to Alice Johnson and Shirley Riley who, as leaders of the Women's International Leadership Conferences, asked me if I would consider putting together this book for those conference gatherings.

To Wes Tracy, *Herald of Holiness* editor and friend, goes my heartfelt thanks for his encouragement, counsel, and insight all along the way.

And to Morris Weigelt, my colleague, soul friend, and fellow pilgrim on the spiritual journey.

Further, I will always be in debt to Terry and Rita Clark, who so generously provided the beauty and solitude of their lakeside home and thus contributed significantly to the completion of the project.

And finally, I am deeply grateful to my wife, Vi, and our two children, Dana and Danny, who encouraged and supported me every step of this journey.

Introduction

In response to requests by friends, I have put together a collection of 31 of the articles on prayer that have appeared in the *Herald of Holiness*. Little did I dream I would ever publish such a book. As I look back on my journey of recent years, I realize it was my mother, now in heaven, who started me on the life of prayer. As a young boy, she encouraged me to replace my "Now I lay me down to sleep" bedtime prayer with the Lord's Prayer. She helped me memorize it, and it grows richer as the years go by. I owe her more than I can express for the spiritual impact she had on my life.

This little book on prayer has been designed to be used in three ways. It can be read straight through, or the reader can choose to read it by the chapters that are of interest at the moment. Finally, it is numbered from 1 to 31 and can be used as a supplement to daily devotions, reading the selection that is the calendar date for that day.

No one could ever hope to write the definitive work on prayer. I trust, however, that you will find in these pages new ways of thinking about and practicing the art of being with God. There are so many unique perspectives and such a variety in prayer that it is an exciting and challenging way to live. With the help of this small book, may you discover the joy, peace, and presence of the risen Christ as you find yourself living in prayer.

I

Prayer of the Heart

*The prayer of the heart is
a prayer of rest.*

HENRI NOUWEN

1 / Heart to Heart

I was . . . er, well . . . stunned, when asked to write on prayer. Cautious and reluctant at first, I finally accepted the invitation. I did not accept because I am a greater prayer, or a saint of the "closet," a writer of readable prayers, or a desert hermit who has had nothing to do but pray since 1940. However, the invitation to share with you what the Lord is teaching me about prayer brought with it an "inner nudge," not a "drive" or an "ought," but a drawing from which I could not run.

I shall approach each topic as a pilgrim, a learner— and oh, how I need to learn! Maybe, in our journey, we can together explore the depths and riches of prayer. I will share with you, and maybe you will be led to share with me. I hope so.

One thing the Lord has taught me about prayer is that it is not the chorelike task I thought it to be when I first found Christ. It appeared to this young Christian that one had to "get hold of God" if prayer was to have any power and receive any response from heaven. And getting hold was not always easy, though it did seem that certain ones had mastered it quite well. This only added to my sense of inadequacy and defeat. I was not sure what "getting hold of God" really meant, but it seemed to include a boisterous intensity that I could not often muster.

But, what if prayer is more a cooperation with God? What if the goal of prayer is not overcoming God's reluctance and obstinance but cooperating with His highest "willingness" for His world? That kind of prayer is vastly superior to my old idea of "getting hold of God" in order to yank Him into my world to get things done on which He seemed reluctant to act. Prayer is bringing myself into an alignment with what He has purposed for me and for those I love.

That kind of accord, or oneness, seems to have been

prominent in the Upper Room when the disciples gathered in obedience to their Lord (Acts 1:14; 2:1). They were in one accord, in one place, praying for the Holy Spirit to come. Isn't that interesting? If I had been there, after all that had happened, what would I have been praying for? With all the arrests, accusations, and crucifixions, I imagine I would have filled my prayer time blubbering over my personal safety. Danger was certainly a factor to be reckoned with.

It's not hard to imagine how I would have prayed concerning the enemies of Jesus, the ones who had so cruelly and unjustly murdered Him. Especially with the injustice of it all wrenching and shattering my spirit. More than likely, I would be memorizing and reciting the imprecatory psalms with both fists clenched: "Consume them in wrath" (59:13); "Do not I hate them, O Lord, that hate thee?" (139:21, KJV).

Surely, there were contingency plans to formulate and God's blessing to be invoked for their success. Plans—just in case; plans to fall back on when all else failed! Plans needed to be laid for getting the gospel out, for expanding the Church.

And then there were the needs of the group. So many needs: loneliness, discouragement, disillusionment. I would pray for those needs.

But *they* didn't; they prayed for *Him*, for the Holy Spirit! Am I anxious to get some gift from the Holy Spirit, or am I determined to get Him? There it is! I've wanted what I thought He wanted to *give* me. But instead He wants me to want *Him*! The gift of himself is the greatest gift that God can give.

Prayer is a person wanting a Person. I'm not praying to get this or that but to get Him, person-to-Person! E. Stanley Jones reminds us that to pray is to penetrate through this physical universe into the spiritual universe.[1] What an awesome privilege! And there are no diplomas or degrees required! It is in prayer that God calls me to cooperate with Him in His divine purposes. I become His partner through prayer.

I spoke earlier of the task of prayer, the burdensome concept that squeezes the vitality from your prayer time. But I hasten to say, prayer, as I have attempted to describe it, is a magnificent and lofty call to responsibility. God is not calling us to chores, tasks, or trivialities, but to partnership with Him. Prayer is, therefore, not to be pursued because it is a task, but because it is so much more important than any *mere* task.

Oswald Chambers said, "The idea of prayer is not in order to get answers from God; prayer is perfect and complete oneness with God."[2] I may not have arrived at that point yet, but now I have a better grasp of the destination. The journey of prayer is person-to-Person, heart-to-heart, face-to-face. I like that; I will seek that. Will you make the journey too?

2 / Pray Without Ceasing

A mystery has haunted my spiritual journey from its very beginning. As a young teen I heard my pastor speak about it, and my Sunday School teachers tried to explain it. Thinking maybe they were stretching it a bit, I looked it up for myself in the Bible—and there it was. "Be joyful always; pray *continually;* give thanks in all circumstances, for this is God's will for you in Christ Jesus" (1 Thess. 5:16-18, italics added). The King James renders it, "Pray without ceasing." No matter how I searched translations, it always came out the same.

Knowing that I did not have time to stay on my knees all day, I assumed it meant something rather general about going at prayer with some consistency, and I left it at that. In fact, in those times when my prayer life seemed to wane and fizzle, I was able to skirt that verse (and others) with consummate skill!

In these later years, I've begun to wonder if maybe there is more to it than I originally thought. Could it be that Jesus and Paul knew something about prayer that I had not yet discovered?

If "ceaseless prayer" is not praying 24 hours a day, then what is it? To begin, even though it is not clock bound, it does have a continuous characteristic about it. Notice that Paul is saying not only that we are to pray *continually*, but also that we are to rejoice *always* and give thanks *in all circumstances*. It is an ongoing characteristic of life, a stance, or a worldview. To John Wesley, this was the threefold mark of those who were wholly sanctified.

There are those who would describe prayer not only as a specific activity but also as an *attitude*.

Many others see prayer more as breathing than as an attitude. They view prayer as the breath in our lungs and the blood in our veins. James C. Fenhagen says, "At the deepest level, prayer is not something we do, but something which the Holy Spirit does in and through us. To say we 'ought' to pray is like saying we ought to breathe. . . . Breathing is a natural part of the life process—the rhythm around which our vital functions are built. So also is the rhythm of prayer."[3]

This view of prayer drives me to go beyond my idea of prayer as a function, to see what it means to "pray without ceasing." It brings me closer to the ideal of a life lived continually in the presence of Jesus. To live in such a way does not remove me from my daily responsibilities, yet neither do the ordinary tasks keep me from Him.

A few days ago I went to a nearby park to read and to think. It was one of those Kansas summer days, hot and breezy. As I sat in the shade, I was aware of the presence of the wind and from time to time took note of it. I also realized that I could go about my reading, walking, talking, or whatever, and still be conscious of the wind. It was always there, and I *knew it,* but that did not keep me from doing other things that needed my attention. In a similar way, ceaseless prayer, lived at the "breathing" level, helps me be aware of His presence all through my day.

There is another description of prayer that is helpful. Life itself is a prayer. Let me explain. I do *not* mean to say that praying on specific occasions is therefore superfluous. But maybe we can integrate the idea of "life as prayer" into our broadening understanding of prayer and see how praying without ceasing is possible.

Various writers have described life as a prayer. For example, W. Bingham Hunter reminds us, "The same idea is found in Paul's 'whatever you do, do it all for the glory of God' (1 Cor. 10:31). This concept, which has deep roots in Judaism, is that one's life is a prayer."[4] And Oswald Chambers says, "Prayer is not an exercise, it is the life."[5]

My mother-in-law, Mable Jahn (now in heaven), was an illustration for me of prayer as the life. If you were around her very long, you began to sense that she and Jesus went everywhere together. Because of her example it is not nearly so hard for me to see life as prayer.

How do I go about "pray[ing] without ceasing"? There are many ways. I can pray when in the midst of a situation with no loss of attention to the task. How often I have prayed for divine wisdom while listening to a counselee (and with my eyes open)! I'm learning to turn my standing-in-line times into opportunities for prayer. I remember Pastor Earl Lee challenging the congregation to make traffic stoplights appointments for prayer. The ways are endless in view of the creative presence of the Holy Spirit!

David Hubbard declares, "Our task is not to get around the commandment but to understand it."[6]

"O God, help me not only to understand it but to live it!"

3 / The Way of Heart Prayer

Praying with the heart is more than just praying. Since we live in a culture that puts a premium on the mind and the senses, it is crucial for us to learn how to pray from the heart. In an intellectually supercharged environment, we are apt to think of prayer as talking to God or thinking about Him. We fall into the trap of making Him a problem to solve or viewing prayer as a practice to perfect. Real prayer, though it may begin at this level, encompasses much more.

Part of our problem lies with the definition of the word "heart." It has been so sentimentalized and prostituted in our day that little of valuable meaning remains. The biblical understanding of heart is much more inclusive and holistic; it is the center or inner being of the person. It includes our mind, will, emotions, desires, hopes, and plans. "Heart" describes who we really are as humans. It is the word used when Jesus said, "Love the Lord your God with all your heart and with all your soul and with all your mind" (Matt. 22:37).

The Psalms teem with references to the heart from a whole-person understanding. For example, "I will extol the Lord with all my heart." "Blessed are they who keep his statutes and seek him with all their heart." "Search me, O God, and know my heart" (111:1; 119:2; 139:23).

The prayer of the heart shows who we really are. It summons us to complete honesty before God. We pray such a prayer, daring to reveal ourselves before the searching light of a holy God. Our cry is that of Isaiah's: "Woe to me! I am ruined!" (6:5). In such moments of transparency, we are open, vulnerable, and desiring nothing but complete surrender. Henri Nouwen says it clearly, "The prayer of the heart challenges us to hide absolutely nothing from God and to surrender ourselves unconditionally to His mercy."[7]

Learning to pray from the heart does not happen overnight. It calls for consistency and patience, leaving the results to God's timing. Two essential ingredients for such a prayer life-style are solitude and silence. Solitude is for being with God, and silence is for listening to Him. Such a quest does not necessarily call for enrollment in a monastery or lengthy separation from life's demands (as helpful and healing as these might be). On the contrary, the challenge is to learn the benefits and skills of silence and solitude in the midst of a busy and noisy world.

Nor is being alone and silent an escape from the cares, worries, and hurts of life. We do not respond to the loving call of the Lord Jesus in order to be exempted from that which normally comes to all of us. We love Him and follow Him and are thereby enabled for living through His Holy Spirit. It is not a matter of *exemption* but of *enablement!*

Therefore, silence and solitude are to be found as rest *in the midst* of all that life brings. I also learned that solitude does not necessarily mean being alone. There is a difference between the creative rest of solitude and a solitude that is loneliness. Solitude with God can be discovered in many ways and places.

As solitude indicates my desire to be *with* God, silence leads me to *listen* to God. Here again, there are countless paths to finding silence in our busy and hectic lives. Silence, solitude, and the prayer of the heart are expressions of intimacy with God. One of the necessary elements for intimacy and a characteristic of heart prayer is attention. It is to be with God and to pay attention. Inattention is one of the deadly enemies of the spiritual life. Attention is not only "seeing" but doing something about what we "see." Referring to Moses and the burning bush, Maxie Dunnam observes: "It is as we go beyond *looking* to *seeing* that we can consciously relate all of life to God. Then we begin to see God as 'the beyond in the midst of life'; we know Him not on the borders but at the center of life."[8]

I am convinced that the journey of prayer is richer, deeper, and more intimate than we may have experienced. If you desire to know God with all your heart, the "prayer of the heart" is worth considering.

4 / Prayer and Meditation

I'm fed up! I'm tired of being cheated out of historical, Christian treasures by witch-hunting pressure groups who see a New Age conspiracy behind every tree. Hitting the bull's-eye with Robin Hood precision, Wes Tracy warned of such thievery and its dire consequences.[9] In that article, he carefully spelled out at least 13 Christian concepts under siege. Why, it's almost to the place where you can't see God in nature, believe in peace, or share a deep, mystical (the dreaded word) experience without being suspected as "one of them."

The art of Christian meditation is one such treasure. I really don't care what transcendentalists or New Agers do with the concept. What saddens me is how little most Christians know about this ancient, biblical path to being with God. How unfortunate for the young student, seeking to know the Christian teaching on meditation, to find that most of the quality writings on the subject are centuries old! No wonder they turn to the East.

Richard Foster, in *Celebration of Discipline,* declares: "It is a sad commentary on the spiritual state of modern Christianity that meditation is a word so foreign to its ears. Meditation has always stood as a classical and central part of Christian devotion, *a crucial preparation for and adjunct to the work of prayer.*"[10]

Meditation is not some 20th-century phenomenon. Called to fill the shoes of Moses, Joshua heard God say, "Do not let this Book of the Law depart from your mouth; meditate on it day and night" (1:8).

From their beginning, the Psalms attest to the joy of commitment to meditation. Speaking of the "blessed" person, the Psalmist says: "His delight is in the law of the Lord, and on his law he meditates day and night" (1:2). In the midst of praising the Lord, the writer prays: "May my

meditation be pleasing to him, as I rejoice in the Lord"
(104:34).

God was no stranger. These ancient people communicated with Him through prayer and meditation as a normal part of life. Hear how eloquently and personally the Psalmist speaks to God: "I remember the days of long ago; I meditate on all your works and consider what your hands have done. I spread out my hands to you; my soul thirsts for you like a parched land" (143:5-6).

What does it mean to meditate? Common definitions include such ideas as contemplate, deliberate, muse, brood, and ruminate.

Historically, for Christians, it has been the listening phase of prayer. It is to approach the object of our meditation without prior judgments. To let go of ego striving and control and hear what is present. Listening is the door to meditative thinking and prayer.

In her book *Pathways of Spiritual Living,* Susan Muto incisively observes: "The meditative stance is not a matter of imposing our thoughts on reality but of attending in quiet vigilance, in gentle reverence, to what is there. Listening reminds us that spiritual formation is first of all a question of receptivity. We cannot give to others what has not already been given to us."[11]

But that is exactly my problem! I have been too prone to try to keep up with my world. The shrill calls to "do more," "be better," and "hurry up" are almost overwhelming. It didn't help to recently hear a prominent TV preacher pronounce that when we feel middle-aged, it's time to DO MORE. No mention of slowing down to listen, to be with the Lord in maturing ways!

Think about what it would take to know God more intimately. I have been challenged to weed out the noise pollution in my life and learn to listen. "May the words of my mouth and the mediation of my heart be pleasing in your sight, O Lord, my Rock and my Redeemer" (Ps. 19:14).

5 / The Practical Discipline

Which of the classical Christian disciplines is the most down-to-earth, the most realistic? Scripture reading? Fasting? Prayer? Journal keeping? None of the above! According to Richard Foster, it is meditation. In *The Celebration of Discipline*, he declares, "Christian meditation leads us to the inner wholeness necessary to give ourselves to God freely, and to the spiritual perception necessary to attack social evils. In this sense it is the most practical of all the Disciplines."[12]

The disciplines common to the Christian church through the ages are quite sensible, contrary to the image our world culture would like to portray. To pray and to meditate is to engage in something that is of cosmic significance and earthly practicality.

Because of various misunderstandings and obstacles, many avoid the practice of meditation. Foster suggests that for some, the art of listening prayer seems too difficult and complicated and therefore should be left to the professionals. Yet it is those very skilled artisans who would shy away from such an idea and declare the practice to be for anyone and everyone. It is a natural part of our Christian heritage and life—meditation and prayer, prayer and meditation.

For others, says Foster, to meditate is to engage in something totally out of touch with our world. They are afraid it will lead to an otherworldliness that is of little use to anyone and insensitive to the world's hurting needs. As a matter of fact, meditation can lead us to deal with life with a focused effectiveness. He reminds us, "It is wonderful when a particular meditation leads to ecstasy, but it is far more common to be given guidance in dealing with ordinary human problems."[13]

Probably the most common reason for not meditating is viewing it as a form of Eastern or New Age religious mumbo jumbo. Nothing could be further from the truth. Where Eastern meditation strives for "emptying," Christian meditation is content-filled. Its purpose is always to bring us to the place where Christ is the Center, where we can more clearly hear Him, know Him, and love Him.

What, then, can we expect when we decide to make meditation and prayer a consistent pattern in our lives? Susan Muto suggests at least five results: (1) we will begin to live a life that is more Christ-centered; (2) imagination, thoughts, decisions, and actions will be broadened and deepened as we minister to our world; (3) we will be able to hear God more clearly in the common, everyday occurrences, rather than expecting to hear Him in the spectacular only; (4) it will help us find patience when the wells seem dry, knowing that God is in the desert too; and (5) we will become more finely tuned instruments, to be used by the Heavenly Father in our world.[14]

If she is right, I need no better reasons for finding a place in my devotional life for meditation. But how do I begin? It is immediately evident that no single technique is going to be the best for everyone. However, some basic guidelines might be helpful.

You will want to find a setting that is conducive to quietness and meditation. There are places in the house that I like much better than others. If it is early in the morning, the den is the best. Before you begin, identify a location.

Next, decide on the material or subject matter for your meditation. It can be a portion of Scripture, a chapter of devotional literature, a segment of your life history, or an issue concerning your future.

When you have chosen the content of your meditation, relax. Read or think about your material. Mull over it, chew on it. Don't let it become work, but let the words speak to you.

Many find memorization, especially of Scripture, to be extremely helpful. As you commit the words to memory, let them sink deep into your mind and heart.

May your meditation and prayer be as natural and as life-giving as breathing itself.

II

Obstacles to Prayer

*The refusal to forgive is one of the
most serious barriers to prayer and health.*

KENNETH LEECH

6 / Forgiveness Is Freedom

As she sat in my office, pouring out her accumulated load of hurt and hatred, she looked at me and with defiance flashing in her eyes said, "I will never forgive him. I can't." My heart sank, for it was like the clanging of a prison door, slamming shut on the freedom God wanted so much to give her. Forgiveness is powerful; forgiveness is freedom.

Forgiveness is central to the Christian faith. Most of us are aware of the impact of forgiveness. We have experienced it and have helped others find it. Many in the mental health professions are coming to see the healing potential in forgiveness. It is one thing to dig into the past, to understand it and face it. It is quite another to let it go, to forgive and be forgiven.

Jesus was never more clear than when He spoke of forgiveness. In Matthew 18, we find the parable of the unmerciful servant. As the story goes, a servant was called to account for a debt he owed his master in the amount of several million dollars. After pleading for mercy, his master canceled the entire amount. He didn't extend it, restructure the payment schedule, or reduce the interest—he wiped it out entirely!

The servant, now free, meets a friend who owes him a few dollars. The friend begs for mercy but instead is thrown into prison (making it even more difficult to pay the paltry loan). When the master heard of it, he pronounced judgment on the servant and in anger imprisoned him. Then the hard words of Jesus, "This is how my heavenly Father will treat each of you unless you forgive your brother from your heart" (Matt. 18:35).

Forgiveness is inextricably tied to prayer. When I come to pray, forgiveness is dealt with, either by conscious choice or by neglect. When God calls me to forgive, it is a serious matter. Jesus said, "And when you stand praying, if you hold anything against anyone, forgive him, so that your Father in heaven may forgive you your sins" (Mark 11:25).

To say that if I want to be forgiven I must forgive, is to make forgiveness a matter of works righteousness. It isn't quite that simple. We forgive out of gratitude for being forgiven. Forgiveness is by grace alone; and those who have been given the grace to forgive deep hurts know it only too well. Rather, Jesus is stating an important reciprocal principle in the economy of God. He is making clear the connection between the prayer and forgiveness. The Psalmist says, "If I had cherished sin in my heart, the Lord would not have listened" (66:18).

To forgive is to set ourselves free. When we forgive, we are released from the "demon" of revenge and bondage to the past. No longer does the past have power over us, nor are we destined to repeat it. Forgiveness shuts off the tape of painful memories. We do not have to continue to play it over and over. We may remember and still forgive. "Forgive and forget" is cruel advice. The miracle is that in the midst of remembering, we are given grace to forgive! Not only do we separate the offender from the offense, but we ourselves are set free as well.

Lewis Smedes, writing in *Christianity Today*, says:

> To forgive is to put down your 50-pound pack after a 10-mile climb up a mountain. To forgive is to fall into a chair after a 15-mile marathon. To forgive is to set a prisoner free and discover that the prisoner was you. To forgive is to reach back into your hurting past and recreate it in your memory so that you can begin again. To forgive is to dance to the beat of God's forgiving heart. It is to ride the crest of love's strongest wave.[1]

To pray, forgiven and forgiving, is to pray in tune with the heart of God! What freedom, what joy!

7 / When Prayer Is Difficult

"It is not part of the life of a natural man to pray. We hear it said that a man will suffer in his life if he does not pray; I question it."[2] So says Oswald Chambers.

Sometimes it *is* difficult to pray. Why is it that sometimes we would rather do just about anything (wash the dishes, work in the yard, straighten the garage, do our homework) than pray? We are Christians, we love the Lord deeply, and yet we struggle to pray. Maybe it's not an issue with you, but it has bothered me more than once!

Many have tried their hand at defining the dilemma. One says that we do not pray for at least five reasons: unbelief, indifference, wrong priorities, a view of prayer as work, or misplaced trust in the things of this world. That may be true for some, but it doesn't help me much.

Another declares that our lack of prayer is a declaration of our self-sufficiency, it is a refusal to appropriate a privilege bought with the blood of Christ, it is a sin against a holy God, and it opens the door to the devil. He explains, "Those of us who have peace with God and access to Him through Christ's blood, and yet do not exercise the privilege purchased by that blood, slap our Lord in the face every time we are guilty of prayerlessness . . . Prayerlessness is a cruel refusal to accept a purchased privilege."[3]

No doubt there is truth here to be considered, but is that all there is? How did Jesus respond to those who slept while He prayed in the Garden of Gethsemane? Certainly, we are not sure how He said the words recorded in the Gospels, "Could you men not keep watch with me for one hour?" (Matt. 26:40). At least there is no indication that He accused them of sinning against a holy God. It is Luke that tells us "he found them asleep, *exhausted from sorrow*" (Luke 22:45, italics added).

There is more than just a law orientation involved in

this problem. There are other reasons worth considering that have been helpful to me.

Gordon MacDonald suggests that prayer is difficult because it seems to be an unnatural activity. It is a tacit admission of our weakness, and there are times when our prayers do not seem to be related at all to the results.[4] That makes sense. Because of the Fall, prayer *is* unnatural for the secularized, self-sufficient person. It *is* difficult for me to admit my weaknesses, when all around me I'm told, "You can be No. 1." And, surely, all of us have prayed with great investment at one time or another, only to wonder why all that effort had such meager results.

Another reason prayer can be difficult is that for the most part, the payoff is in the future. With the bank, the house payment, the car, and utilities, it's the first of the month, *every month!* But who will call us to accountability on a regular basis in this matter of prayer? Days go by, weeks pass into months without prayer, and our world has not come to an end. It isn't until later we realize the result of our neglect is the slow withering of our friendship with God.

The unwillingness to forgive can also keep us from our appointment with God. Jesus made it rather clear in more than one place that forgiveness was crucial. Kenneth Leech was right when he said, "The refusal to forgive is one of the most serious barriers to prayer and health."[5]

I believe for many, difficulty in prayer is not because of laziness or rebellion, but because the issues are becoming clearer and more demanding. No longer is prayer an "activity," one of the things I "do" in order to be a good Christian. Now I'm faced with an Almighty God, who is calling me to radical obedience, and it "ain't" always comfortable! Henri Nouwen put it this way:

> Although we often feel a real desire to pray, we experience at the same time a strong resistance. We want to move closer to God, the source and goal of our existence, but at the same time we realize that the

closer we come to God the stronger will be his demand
to let go of the many "safe" structures we have built
around ourselves.[6]

So, prayer is difficult sometimes because we are rebel-
lious, disobedient, or lazy. But prayer can also be tough
because it is significant. When we pray, God reaches to
the depths of our spirits and invites us to be more like His
Son. We are dealing with a Person, one who loves us and
wants us to love and obey Him in an ever-deepening relationship. If you are struggling to pray, it is not the time to
give up. Maybe it is the way the Heavenly Father is getting
us to face the real issues in our prayer lives.

Oswald Chambers finishes the quote I started with by
saying, "What will *suffer* is the life of the Son of God in
him, which is nourished not by food, but by prayer."[7]
Prayer is not the only thing I can do, but it is the most important thing I can do.

8 / Prayer and the Cloud of Darkness

I believe many Christians at one time or another find
themselves in a cloud of darkness. Some call it depression. Whatever the term, it has many manifestations and
comes from various causes. Certainly it is no stranger to
the family of God.

Who encounters the cloud of darkness? Surely Elijah
felt the impact of the cloud of darkness after his great vic-
tory on Mount Carmel. After receiving the death threat
from Jezebel, the Bible says, "Elijah was afraid and ran for
his life. . . . He came to a broom [juniper, KJV] tree, sat
down under it and prayed that he might die. 'I have had
enough, Lord,' he said. 'Take my life; I am no better than
my ancestors'" (1 Kings 19:3-4).

Typical of someone suffering this condition, his percep-

tion was distorted. A few verses later he tells God that he is
the only faithful one left. The Lord reminds him that there
are actually 7,000 in Israel who have remained faithful.

The two disciples on the road to Emmaus in Luke 24
were certainly victims of the cloud of darkness. Their
hopes had been brutally shattered by the Crucifixion. "But
we had hoped," one of them responded to Jesus (v. 21).
Their body language was characteristic: "They stood still,
their faces downcast" (v. 17). Hope was gone and vision
blurred. So heavy was the dark cloud, it took a consider-
able amount of time before they recognized Jesus, who
walked and talked with them.

Finally, and with the greatest of reverence, let us consider the experience of Jesus in the Garden of Gethsemane. The Scriptures tell us, "He began to be sorrowful and
troubled" (Matt. 26:37). It is variously translated as "began to show grief and distress of mind and was deeply depressed" (Amp.), "anguish and dismay came over him"
(NEB), "began to give way to His grief and distress of
heart" (Williams), "began to be in terrible distress and
misery." I would suggest that Jesus was having to pray in
the midst of the cloud of darkness.

What causes the cloud of darkness experience? One
thing we learn when we study about this dark cloud experience is that it is far too complex for any generalizing or
simple answers. Dr. Archibald D. Hart, dean of the School
of Psychology of Fuller Theological Seminary, is helpful in
pointing out some faulty ideas of this malady that are
common in the church today.

Some believe that depression is the result of sin. This
is certainly not new nor totally false. Job received the
same advice. It is not helpful, however, when radio and
TV preachers leave the impression that *all* depression is
sin-related. It simply is not true.

Others would hold that this dark cloud is the result of a
lack of faith. It is distressing when a prominent biblical ex-

positor writes, "We can indeed sum it all up by saying that the final and ultimate cause is just sheer unbelief." Such words are not only lacking in real help for many, Hart believes, but for some caught in the cloud, they are hurtful.[8]

What then are we to do if we find the cloud of darkness affecting our lives? First, we can remember that God is still in control. He understands where we are and what is happening to us. He understands our Gethsemane.

Second, we can hope. It is hope made real by the gospel, the death and resurrection of our Lord! It is the risen Christ who stands near when the cloud overwhelms, and it is He who calls us out of it.

Third, we can pray. And if the cloud is too dark, we can find friends who will help carry our stretcher and lower us through the roof to Jesus when we cannot help ourselves. The Psalmist points the way. "Why are you downcast, O my soul? Why so disturbed within me? Put your hope in God, for I will yet praise him, my Savior and my God" (42:5-6).

9 / In Search of the Quiet Place

There are moments in the busyness of my days when I feel as if I am unraveling at the edges. My breath comes in short spurts, and my fingers cannot seem to grasp or work with as much precision as before. I drop things, knock things over, fumble with things.

My mind races, trying to think time into a standstill. I doubt the basic goodness God has created in me as a redeemed human being. I call myself all manner of names to describe my failure and unworthiness. If I can't get organized, if I can't control time, then what good am I? How can I ever be successful? I finally get everything together and make it to my next appointment—barely on time!

Similar scenarios with basically the same emotional impact are all too common to us. We find ourselves off-balance, disoriented, and confused. There is a time for everything, and there is a time when finding the quiet place is crucial. Our challenge is to go beyond the tyranny of time, to be free of its grip, rather than to utilize its pressure as a rationalization for not praying. In properly thinking of time, we reject the flurry of our age and believe with the biblical writers that there is a time and a season for everything (Eccles. 3:1-8).

As prayer becomes a natural part of living, time loses its iron grasp, its tyrannical influence. With Ted Loder, we can pray for the "unclenched moment." In his book of prayers, he writes:

> Guide me,
> Holy One,
> into an unclenched moment,
>   a deep breath,
>   a letting go
>   of heavy expectancies,
>   of shriveling anxieties,
>   of dead certainties,
> that, softened by the silence,
>   surrounded by the light,
>   and open to the mystery,
> I may be found by wholeness,
>   upheld by the unfathomable,
>   entranced by the simple,
>   and filled with the joy
>   that is you.[9]

Susan Muto points out several barriers to this style of quiet prayer. It isn't as easy as it sounds. For one thing, sheer human pride has a way of blocking the doorway to this spiritual pathway. When I come to pray, it is the self that can be my undoing. To pray is to humbly and completely open myself to God. Pride leads me to use prayer as a way of getting God's OK on my plans and projects rather than as an avenue of surrender to His will for me.

More subtle still, pride can lead to the temptation to see my success as evidence that prayer "works." The more I possess and the more I succeed, the more powerful are my prayers. To pray because prayer works can be spiritually dangerous.

Another hurdle to a life of prayerful presence is our inclination to avoid the way of the Cross. Our culture is obsessed with feeling good, so spirituality can become equated with the same sort of emotional good times! We find ourselves inept and unwilling to cope with life as it comes, to see the divine hand at work in the rotten deals of life. We are either unwilling or unable to see the difficulties of life as opportunities for profound spiritual growth.

Muto suggests as a third obstacle our inability to wait. How strenuous and aggravating it is for us to wait for anything—for our groceries, for the doctor, for the stoplight, for God. Frustration simmers while we wait for something to transpire over which we have little or no influence. We miss the chance to use such moments as opportunities for prayer.[10]

How different it is when we find the "prayer of the quiet place." We sit down with God and, in the quiet, let Him fill our space with His presence. We are renewed, energized, loved, healed. Prayer becomes joyful, relaxed, with no drivenness, no competition.

If you have yet to experience this kind of gentle prayer, I invite you to find *your* quiet place. Explore what it can mean to just "be" in His presence, engulfed by His love and renewed for your world. May you find your "unclenched moment."

III

The Question of Unanswered Prayer

We are not here to prove God answers prayer; we are here to be living monuments of God's grace.

OSWALD CHAMBERS

10 / And the Silence Is Deafening

One of the great mysteries of prayer is the issue of praying to a silent God. Aligned with this struggle are the moments when our prayers do not seem to match the results. How often as a pastor I would come to the end of a Sunday service bewildered. At times the service and its impact would seem to be far beyond what I had prayed and worked toward. On other occasions, I would anticipate a service built on hours of prayer and preparation, only to have it fall flat and lifeless at my feet.

There are times when I pray and the silence of God seems deafening. Why is He silent? Why doesn't He answer? What torturous questions these can be!

At least we know the questions are not new. The story of Job provides a vivid picture of such anguish. In the midst of his agony, he cries: "Even today my complaint is bitter; his hand is heavy in spite of my groaning. If only I knew where to find him; if only I could go to his dwelling! . . . But if I go to the east, he is not there; if I go to the west, I do not find him. When he is at work in the north, I do not see him; when he turns to the south, I catch no glimpse of him" (23:2-3, 8-9).

Where *is* God when I need Him? Why *doesn't* He answer? Ever been plagued by those kinds of thoughts? Most of us have. Some concepts have been helping me in recent days. Maybe they will be of help to you also.

To begin with, I need to reorient my thinking and praying to the fact that what I am really after is God and His presence, not things. So often we try to get God to pull something off for us, to work things out, when what we really need is Him! Somehow I must come to understand that God is not a cosmic vending machine, dispensing my every desire as long as I follow the right formula! Early on I picked up the idea that praying was "asking." "Ask and it will be given to you; seek and you will find; knock and the door will be opened to you" (Matt. 7:7). The startling question is: Do I love God *for* God or for what I can get from Him?

The Gethsemane drama hits home at this point. In that moving scene in Luke 22, what does Jesus pray for? Facing persecution, humiliation, and execution, He prays that His will will be aligned with the will of the Father. "Not my will, but thine, be done" (v. 42, KJV). Now, what would we have prayed for?

I remember the days when our children would come in boldness to ask for something. Sometimes the request was easily answered. At other times it took careful thought. As a father, my desire was to answer in the affirmative if at all possible. But I shall never forget the day, following a rich time together, when one of them said, "Dad, it's just good to be with you." I need to learn more of what it means to "be with" my Heavenly Father.

Anthony Bloom suggests some ways of looking at the silence of God. First is the idea that prayer is relationship. This relationship is characterized by mutuality. If that is so, then God could just as easily complain about me when I complain about Him. When it comes to the few occasions I resent or am bewildered by His silence, He could just as easily recall the countless times I have been silent toward Him. I look for Him in the 15 to 30 minutes I have allotted for such an encounter and complain when He is not there. He, then, could rightly call me to account for the other 23½ hours when He has wanted to be with me, but I have been too busy. As Bloom suggests, maybe we have no right to complain about His absence when we are absent far more frequently than He is.

Further, think about how we pray. What about those moments when our prayers are intense, on fire, determined? Does it not pertain to some subject over which we are greatly concerned, a loved one, something of deep importance to us? And when we move on in our praying and the fervor is not as obvious, has God changed? No, it is the fact that our intensity was centered on the subject of our praying, not on Him. It is that I am still determined to *get* something from Him. Could it be that unanswered prayer is His invitation to discover my adequacy in Him and not what He can give me?[1]

Lloyd Ogilvie sums it up when he says:

> What seems to be unanswered prayer is also a part of His instigation and invitation to communion and conversation with Him on a deeper level. He wants us to know Him more profoundly than ever. When we feel our prayers are not answered according to our specifications and timing, that feeling is really a longing for God and not just for what He can give or do for us. Thank God for those times. By them we know we have been called into a much more intimate relationship than we've ever known before![2]

11 / The Mysteries of Unanswered Prayer

"Have you ever felt as if God did not hear you when you prayed?" That was the question a group of students was dealing with in a class on preparation for ministry. "Yes," the student shared, "when my mother died of cancer." Her mother had been diagnosed with a fast-growing tumor and had been given just months to live. Her mother's one wish was that she could live until the holidays (some seven months away) to be able to have one last Christmas with her children.

This wish became the center of prayers of the family and the student for the following months. It was such a reasonable, humane, Christian request. "O God, please let her live so that she can at least enjoy one last Christmas, Your Son's birthday, with her family." She died that *Christmas Eve.*

I sat stunned. Surely, this was a made-up story, a script for some sick television show. But no, it was for real! None of us were surprised as the student related her long battle with the validity of prayer after that crushing experience.

Have *you* ever prayed and wondered why God did not answer? If you have, you are certainly not alone. This is one of those "heavy" questions about prayer.

I have come face-to-face with the issue in my own life. I have had some level of headache pain every day of my life since I was 16 years old and a sophomore in high school. Most of the time they are tolerable with medication, but sometimes they become migraines and totally immobilize me. When that happens, it takes 24 to 48 hours for the pain to subside and another day to recover from the physical effects of the constant pain.

I have prayed for years that I might be released from my headaches. How much more effective I could be for my Lord, how much more productive, let alone more civil to everyone around me! Surely that would be in God's will— to make me as proficient a minister as possible. But that prayer has not yet been answered after these 40 years.

I've been to every doctor imaginable, this clinic and that. I've been hooked up to machines, poked with needles, and taken every test I can think of. No answer, only pain. I've been prayed for and anointed for healing. No answer, just continuous pain. I believe in healing prayer. I have practiced it in public and in private. But for this malady of mine, there seems to have been no answer.

In recent days I have had to face the possibility of another physical adjustment in my life, one that is not terminal, but neither can it be cured. It may call for a new look at how I do the physical things that for years I so took for granted.

Now how do I face this new development in my life? How do I go about praying to a God who seemingly has not answered the one continuous prayer of my life, to be made free of my headache pain? Should I bring this new situation to Him? Can I trust Him with this new area of supplication? What if there is no answer? What if He remains silent?

In recent years, I have become committed to some principles or understandings in this area. Along with these principles I want to share some other suggestions that might prove helpful in this often confusing and sometimes excruciating quest for answers.

The first principle to which I am committed and upon which I rest my faith is this: *For God's children, ALL prayers are answered!* Not some but not others, not the ones where I have "enough faith," or where I have persevered long enough to qualify for an answer, but . . . ALL of them! You will notice throughout this discussion I have said, *seemed* to be no answers. Spend some time with this one thought: *For God's children, ALL prayers are answered.* What difference would it make if you really believed it was true?

12 / Facing Unanswered Prayer

We have raised the specter of "unanswered" prayer, that unsettling possibility that most of us have encountered at one time or another. What do we do when God seems silent? What do we think when our prayers seem to go unheeded, even after months and possibly years of perseverance?

Over the passage of time, I have come to some basic assumptions and beliefs that have guided my prayer journey, and I want to share them with you.

A foundational principle is the belief that, for God's children, ALL prayers are answered! This statement hits at the heart of what it means to pray. Prayer is communication. It is dialogue with the Eternal God, the Creator of the Universe, who wants to have fellowship with *me!* I pray in order to commune with God, to talk to Him, to be in His presence, and to *know Him*. When I pray, I seek *Him*.

Lloyd Ogilvie forcefully says:

> There is a great difference between unanswered prayer and ungranted petitions. Wishing is not real praying. We could have our wants granted and not have received an answer to prayer. The purpose of prayer is communion and conversation with God. The period of waiting for the granting of some request is often rewarded by a far greater gift than what we asked for. The Lord himself. What is delayed or denied is according to a much greater plan and wisdom than we possess in our finite perception.[3]

I have mentioned my years of headache pain with no apparent answer to many a request for deliverance. As I reflected on that journey, I have come to realize that God has given more than just pain relief! He has given himself—*when I have been willing to receive Him*. Especially in recent years, my friendship with God has grown deeper and richer than ever before. The pain, though an unwelcome guest, has become a reminder of my need for Him. He is my Source and my Strength, regardless of what is happening to me.

Resting on the belief that God faithfully answers all prayer, there are several possible ways of looking at those times when God does not seem to be listening. Many have written on the subject of obstacles or hindrances to prayer and have suggested that one of God's answers is no. This could be for various reasons.

It might be that the request itself is wrong. We are certainly not the first to approach the Lord with an inappropriate supplication. As recorded in Matthew and Mark, James and John asked to be given seats at the Lord's right and left hand. The answer was no. Their request was definitely out of line.

When we come to our Heavenly Father with inappropriate requests, He loves us too much to allow us to have that which might ultimately do us irreparable harm. He also knows when our motives are askew, and then He must say no. When I pray, asking God for His help, what am I *really* praying for and, even more important, *why* am I making this request? So, not only the request but also our motives can be wrong.

Bill Hybels suggests that before bringing a request to God it would be a good idea to ask the following questions: If God granted this request, would it bring glory to Him? Would it advance His kingdom? Would it help people? Would it help me grow spiritually? Stopping long enough to honestly examine the way I pray has helped me pray with more integrity and more assurance.[4]

There is still more to be said about the question of unanswered prayer. For now, consider the following challenge from Lloyd Ogilvie: "The personal and practical application to all this is that when prayers seem unanswered, take it as a signal that the Lord wants to help us discover our sufficiency in Him and not what He can give us in tangible blessings."[5]

13 / Living with Unanswered Prayer

In discussing the irksome problem of unanswered prayer, we have assumed that for God's children, ALL prayers are answered. When attempting to discern why some prayers seem to go unanswered, I proposed that one reason might very well be that the request itself is wrong. In that case, the answer is no, as well it should be.

Another reason for a seeming delay in answered prayer may have to do with the timing of our requests. As Lloyd Ogilvie suggests, these "unanswered prayers . . . may not be best for us or are not in keeping with the Lord's timing for us."[6] How many of us, when looking back, can see how our requests, if they had been answered in the way we prayed and intended, would have produced anything but the desired result! We can see it clearly now, but at the time it seemed as if skies were slate and God was silent.

Bill Hybels proposes that the timing may be off for several good reasons. It could be a time to test our faith. How are we relating to our Heavenly Father? Are we pushing for *our* request or are we willing to wait for the Father to answer in His own way and time? One sign a child is maturing is the ability to wait for, to postpone, the answer to a request of a parent. It is one thing for a two-year-old to scream and stomp for something "now." It may be annoying or uncomfortable when we see it while shopping, for example, but we may understand it based on age. It is quite another matter when encountering a teen with the same behavior patterns! Then it becomes sad.

Further, a delay may be for the development of character and qualities that might not come to pass any other way. Many believe as Hybels, that God sometimes delays to help us develop endurance, trust, patience, or submission. A lot of spiritual growth comes by way of pain, hurt, struggle, confusion, and disappointment. Hybels asks, "If we had our way, though, how long would any of us put up with these character builders without asking God to remove them?"[7]

Finally, prayers may seem to go unanswered because there is something wrong with us. Many writers have addressed this subject, and the suggestions are numerous. One of the most devastating conditions for effective praying is when there is unresolved relational conflict. How powerful are Jesus' words when He says: "Therefore, if you are offering your gift at the altar and there remember that your brother has something against you, leave your gift there in front of the altar. First go and be reconciled to your brother; then come and offer your gift" (Matt. 5:23-

24). There stands the penetrating truth, and rather than explaining it away, I had best take my hat off to it and say, "Good morning"!

The Book of James provides some interesting insights into the roadblocks to effective prayer. In the very first chapter, verses 5-8, doubt is pinpointed as a possible problem. When we ask, we are to believe and not doubt. Otherwise we end up double-minded and should not expect to get anything from the Lord. James really starts toe stomping in chapter 4, verses 2 and 3. "You do not have, because you do not ask God. When you ask, you do not receive, because you ask with wrong motives, that you may spend what you get on your pleasures."

How painfully embarrassing it has been in my life to discover I had been fretting and stewing over a major issue and had not *really* prayed about it! Has that ever happened to you?

We have talked about requests that are wrong and the answer is "No," those that are out of timing and the answer is "Wait," and supplications that come when we are out of kilter and the answer is "Mature." In response to this problem of effective prayer, Calvin Miller says, "First, we should feel complete freedom to ask a loving Father for the desires of our heart. Second, we must agree that what we want can be set aside to meet the demands of a higher will. Third, our ultimate motivation for prayer should not be that we want something from God but that we want God."[8]

14 / Beyond Unanswered Prayer

We have mentioned various possibilities that might result in a lack of prayer "success." One more needs to be considered. It is the suggestion that there are times when we pray for things we should take care of ourselves. In those situations, it is not a time for prayer but a time for action.

How easy it is to pray for something to happen and to mean it with all our hearts. But when we get honest about it, we realize God is telling us to get moving, take care of it, get involved! Suppose my son came to me, asking that I do his homework for him so that he could do something else. What kind of father would I be to let him get away with such a strategy, no matter how sincere he was? The *best* thing for him is not to answer his request but get him involved in what *he* can do. It may take some encouragement and support, but *he* must do it to reap the greatest benefit.

So, it could be that some of my seemingly "unanswered" prayers are a call for me to do what *I* can do and no doubt *should* do. The answer to this prayer, then, is to give to God my very best, to be used and empowered by His Spirit, as He sees fit.

Let's conclude with some basic principles.

First, I have been saying right along that, "For God's children, ALL prayers are answered." In one way or another, God hears, God listens, and God answers, whether I catch on or not! The answer may be "No," and that puts an end to it. It may be that the request is ill-timed, and the answer is "Wait." Or it could be that there is something wrong with my attitude, and then the answer is "Grow up."

A second principle or assumption is that God is sovereign. He does as He wills, including answering my prayers! Yes, He is Love, but He is also sovereign Lord of the universe. Ultimately, then, I have to come to terms with the fact that, not only will my prayers be answered, but they will be answered His way, and in the way *best* for me! The life of Jesus illustrates over and over a loving Father's care for His children. But in Gethsemane, even Jesus came face-to-face with God's will and plan. In that anguished moment, He was able to pray, "Abba, Father, . . .

everything is possible for you. Take this cup from me. Yet not what I will, but what you will" (Mark 14:36).

That prayer leads me to the third principle. In the final analysis, "Thy will be done" is the highest prayer I can pray. God answers all prayer. God not only is sovereign but also wants the very best for me. Therefore, "Thy will be done!" Easy to say, but difficult to do, right? Part of the reason is this kind of prayer requires complete submission and total surrender. As noted earlier, we are not talking here about a "vending machine" God who dispenses product based upon the amount of "prayer coin" inserted! To be faithful in prayer, and yet be willing to accept God's will in the case, no matter what, is to move toward maturity.

Of course, this kind of response to God can be filled with resignation and fatalism. That leads to despair and depression. But to pray it in hope, the hope founded on the resurrection of Jesus Christ and in a God who wills the very best for us, is to pray victoriously!

The headaches I have mentioned before are a case in point. They have been with me a long time. I pray faithfully for healing. But more than that, I pray that I will be able to discern God's action and will in it all. "In all things God works for the good of those who love him, who have been called according to his purpose" (Rom. 8:28). God is sovereign, He answers all prayer, Thy will be done!

Archibald Hart sums it up in *15 Principles for Achieving Happiness* by saying: "Praying this prayer gives you a significant opportunity for growth in your relationship with God. After all, God will do His will whether or not we pray 'Thy will be done.' But praying this way opens up our minds and hearts to following Him. *We* are the losers if we cannot do it."[9]

IV

Silence and Prayer

*We need to find God, and He cannot be
found in noise and restlessness.*

MOTHER TERESA

15 / How Can You Pray with a Noisy Heart?

Have you ever "felt" the silence? It can happen in those serendipitous moments when all clatter and clanging around us suddenly give up, and you almost "feel" the silence. For some, such silence is a consolation to the soul, a healing for a shattered spirit. For others, such absence of noise becomes threatening and even terror-filled.

Ours is a noisy world. Even as I write late in the afternoon, the noises find their way into my office sanctuary. A vacuum is roaring away as it devours the dirt and grime from a hallway carpet. Traffic hums and swooshes its frantic way past my window. Voices from another office force their way through the walls. Wherever I go in my world, there is noise: radio, television, traffic, people.

No wonder our hearts are noisy too. How can they be otherwise? Our younger generation appears to be "wired for sound." Whether walking, skateboarding, driving, or studying, they are not far from noise. Most of the time they are immersed in it. Sound engulfs their minds and souls through earphones that are barely visible.

While the young may have their challenges with technology and music, I find that I live in a world made noisy by words. I deal so much with words that they can clutter up my mind and heart with noise. Not only so, but also the words themselves can become empty, drained of their meaning. Henri Nouwen, talking about us religious teacher types, reminds us: "When our words are no longer a reflection of the divine Word in and through whom the world has been created and redeemed, they lose their grounding and become as seductive and misleading as the words used to sell Geritol."[1]

How God comes to us in silence is accented in the fascinating story of Elijah found in 1 Kings 19:9-12. Elijah waits for God outside his mountain retreat. Three astounding events happen. First, Elijah encounters a rock-splitting wind, then comes a ground-shattering earthquake, and finally an earth-scorching fire. Surely God would appear in at least one of those cataclysms! What a dramatic and "Godlike" entrance. But instead, the Lord of heaven is discovered in—a whisper. A whisper! A still, small voice.

When we are encouraged by Scripture to "be still, and know that I am God" (Ps. 46:10), we ought to pay attention. To be still is not all that easy, but it *is* possible. Even Jesus found it necessary to get away from those around Him and be *alone*.

We know that silence can mean "the absence of noise," but it is also instructive to know that there are differences between "noise" and "noise." Researchers say that there is a difference between the decibels generated by heavy city traffic and the same level of decibels created by a waterfall. My neighbor's rackety lawn mower impacts my spirit in a different way than the morning chorus of chickadees and cardinals in the trees nearby. If it's morning, I awake in a different mood to that lawn mower's growl than I do to my feathered friends singing!

We need to consider not only the sounds that are healthy and creative but also the possibility that our hearts and our life-styles need periods of worshipful silence.

I say worshipful, for some silences are deadly. The growing silence between estranged marriage partners and the sudden silence of a teen contemplating suicide are deadly silences.

I can be silent enough to hear God "in a whisper." When I ask myself certain questions, I begin to discover where the possibilities are for more quietness in my life. For example, in my daily schedule, where is that one time or place that provides the opportunity for silence? In recent months, that time for me has been just after rising in the morning, before anyone else in the family is awake. With no reading or radio or activity of any kind, I sit and "soak up the silence." It gives my noisy heart a chance to begin the day quietly—with God.

Are there any "islands" of silence in my day that I might be overlooking? How's my progress in weaning myself away from the incessant noises of television, radio, and the stereo? As I ask these questions and others, I'm made aware and encouraged that there are some ways to deal with my noisy heart.

When noise and words dominate my life, then my prayers can drift into nothing more than performances for God. Henri Nouwen says it best in *The Living Reminder:* "Thinking about my own prayer, I realize how easily I make it into a little seminar with God . . . thinking profound thoughts and saying impressive words. I am obviously still worried about the grade!"[2] It is when I am learning how to be quiet and "still" that I begin to discover the depths and riches of "knowing God."

16 / Solitude and Prayer

In recent days, the idea of solitude and prayer has pushed its way into my thinking. Solitude is easier for some than it is for others, but the Scriptures indicate that this practice is important for all of us. While instructing His disciples in Matt. 6:5-8, Jesus said, "When you pray, go into your room, close the door and pray to your Father, who is unseen" (v. 6). During His powerful public ministry, He also practiced solitude at crucial moments.

In preparation for His life's mission, He spent 40 days alone in the desert (Matt. 4:1-11). When needing wisdom in choosing the Twelve, He spent the night alone (Luke 6:12). He chose a lonely mountain for the Transfiguration

(Matt. 17:1-2). It was a long and lonely night in the Garden of Gethsemane (26:36-44). After feeding 5,000, He went to a mountain to be by himself (14:23). In Luke 5:16, He withdrew to lonely places. After a long night of work, He rose early and went to a solitary place (Mark 1:35).

What a dissonant topic for people like us. We are *so* busy. There is so much to do that seldom do we find periods in which we do not know what needs to be done next. We are so swept along by the "musts" and "oughts" of life that there is no time to wonder if all that we do is *worth* doing.

Why is solitude so important? First, it is the place where we meet our Lord, to be with Him. The reason for being alone is found in 1 John 1:1, "That which was from the beginning, which we have heard, which we have seen with our eyes, which we have looked at and our hands have touched—this we proclaim concerning the Word of life." If I want that level of fellowship with my Lord, I will have to be responsible in creating moments of solitude. My society certainly will not give it to me!

Second, in solitude I find that prayer is not valuable because "it works" but because there is value in prayer itself. To commune with the risen Christ, to be *with* Him is far more valuable than all the "results" of prayer, as blessed as they may be.

Third, it is in solitude that I begin to evaluate my world with more clarity and discernment. This materialistic society tries its best to convince me that what I own is how much I'm worth, and who I am is to be evaluated on the basis of what I do. Henri Nouwen puts it so clearly, "It is in this solitude that we discover that being is more important than having, and that we are worth more than the result of our effort."[3]

There is a subtle trap here. To be alone with God is not all there is to the transforming Christian journey; it is only a part of it. In reality, those who find time to be alone with the Lord find heightened sensitivities to the suffering, the poor, and the marginal among us. Nouwen reminds us, "In and through solitude we do not move away from people. On the contrary, we move closer to them through compassionate ministry."[4]

What are some ways into solitude, in the midst of our jam-packed schedules and frenetic lives? One thing you can do is find a place of quiet that is right for you. Where in your home is an area that can be made into your "solitary place"? What about the "moments of solitude" that dot our days? Mine has been the early morning before the family is up, but they occur throughout the day if I look for them. Have you considered personal retreats throughout the year? They may be hours or days, out of the city or in a quiet corner of the public library. The options are many.

Solitude helps put our world into perspective. I've often wondered why the Church does not seem to make more of a difference in the world. Maybe our impotence in changing the world is due, in part, to our addiction to the world. Solitude with the living Lord can help break that addiction.

17 / The Listening Prayer

Sometimes we talk too much. That is especially the case when we pray. But prayer is not meant to be a one-way street. Rather, it is a dialogue with the Almighty, and dialogue demands listening as much as talking. But listening involves silence, and that isn't easy. Being silent even for a little while can be an awesome challenge in these days.

The Bible writers knew about silence. Habakkuk declared pointedly, "The Lord is in his holy temple; let all the earth be silent before him" (2:20). The Psalmist proclaimed the word of the Lord, "Be still, and know that I am God" (46:10).

How noisy is our world! We are hit with messages from every corner of our existence. It reminds me of standing in an airport, hearing the incessant alarm of the passenger tram working its way through the milling bodies, the ever-present announcements of impending flights, calls for persons who should report here and there, and the clatter and din of voices, noisy luggage racks, and bustling people.

Our cars provide little refuge, for there are the millions of words that seductively call out to us from the highway billboards. The radio beckons us to buy this and join that. In our world of noise, words begin to lose their meaning. Learning to be silent can help restore their power.

Calvin Miller says, "The listening prayer is a prayer of relationship. It is listening silence, shouting silence but silence nonetheless. . . . Hearing God in our devotion keeps Him from being a mute deity. . . . The Almighty wants us to be open to Him. Our silence is a door for Him to enter."[5] Could that be a reason why some have difficulty believing that God "is there"?

Jesus' ministry involved the crowds and also the times of solitude. How often He felt the need to be alone and silent, especially at crucial times. If Jesus needed the strength and empowerment of silence and solitude over and over again, how much more do we need to find them in our lives. Wayne Oates suggests several questions to get at this idea of creating silence. He asks:

> Have you caught yourself becoming fatigued, losing perspective, exercising poor judgment, and becoming confused? Did you immediately create some time of silence for yourself? What initiative have you taken to create specific times, places, and rituals for privacy and solitude? Have you stood apart, backed off, turned aside, and broken out from your noisy overin-

volvement to experience silence? Are you aware of the silent Presence of God in any personal way at all?[6]

Not only does our world tend to drown out the voice of God within, but also our own intercessions and pain can muffle and obscure the fact that the Heavenly Father is speaking. I wonder how many times in my personal strife and pain I have prayed, thinking God was not even listening, when all the time my attention was so much on my personal crisis that I could not hear Him? Silence, though not easy, can help me hear His still, small voice in the midst of my noisy world.

Begin to look for those "pockets" of silence in your day, at work, at home, at school. Let them become moments of creative, hallowed, "listening prayer."

V

Praying the Scriptures

*This kind of prayer gets you out of
the way so that God's Word can
edify you, heal you, restoring you
to the person He wants you to be.*

LEONARD LeSOURD

18 / How to Pray the Scriptures

Praying the Scriptures can bring new depths of devotion, communication, and creativity to our walk with the Lord. It is a way of praying practiced by many. Some might call it "praying the Word of God." It can open new vistas of knowledge about the Bible and can enrich our relationship with God.

Praying the Scriptures is a way of using portions of the Bible as the framework for our talk with the Lord. Appropriate phrases and sentences that can be used abound on nearly every page! The Psalms are especially helpful and readily lend themselves to this kind of praying. When we pray the Psalms, we discover praise and thanksgiving richly expressed. During those times when my praying becomes repetitive and hackneyed, the Psalms can bring life to my lackluster prayers.

In addition, when I pray the Psalms or any other portion of Scripture, I can know I am praying in God's will. It adds confidence and boldness where before there may have lurked fear and uncertainty.

Some portions of God's Word lend themselves directly to prayer, without much need for personalizing. They immediately become my personal request. For example,

Create in me a pure heart, O God, and renew a steadfast spirit within me. Do not cast me from your presence or take your Holy Spirit from me. Restore to me the joy of your salvation and grant me a willing spirit, to sustain me *(Ps. 51:10-12)*.

Other sections need only minor paraphrasing or simple changes in wording to make them my own.

O Lord, I praise you that you are my shepherd! I have all I need! You make me to lie down in green pastures, you lead me beside quiet waters, you calm and restore my soul. Please lead me in the paths of righteousness for your name's sake *(Ps. 23:1-3, paraphrased)*.

Not only the Psalms but other portions of God's Word can be prayed in this manner. When I want to deepen my adoration and praise, I look to the first chapter of Colossians:

> O Lord, I praise you that you are the firstborn over all creation, that all things were created by you. It doesn't matter what it was, things in heaven or on earth, visible or invisible, thrones, powers, rulers, or authorities, all things were created by you! In you everything holds together! *(vv. 15-17, paraphrased).*

When we pray for others, we can pray the Scriptures by personalizing it for them. I have found this a powerful way to pray for my children. For example:

> O Lord, I know you are Dana's shepherd! With you, she will have need of nothing. Lead her beside still waters today. Restore her soul and lead her in the paths of righteousness . . . *(Psalm 23, paraphrased).*

Or when praying for our teenage son:

> O God, bless Danny today as he refuses to walk in the counsel of the wicked or stand in the way of sinners or sit in the seat of mockers. As he walks with you, let him delight in your law, bring it to his memory today *(Ps. 1:1-2, paraphrased).*

The possibilities are endless; and in praying the Scriptures, my Bible becomes more and more a vital part of my prayer life.

Leonard E. LeSourd, in *Touching the Heart of God,* suggests another method of scriptural praying.

> Try, for example, the story of the woman caught in adultery (John 8:2-11). First, read it through and ask God to reveal what His teaching is for you in these verses. Next, read the words again slowly, prayerfully. Linger on those words that seem meant for you. Do you identify with the accusers? the sinner? both? neither?
>
> Then listen. What is God saying? Let yourself be like a child nestled in God's lap, listening to His words.
>
> Last, *let Him take over.* Let Him love you. Let Him console you. Let Him forgive you.[1]

What power there is in praying the Word of God! If you have not tried this rich path to prayer, why not now? Open the Scriptures, and then be prepared to open your heart to the healing presence of the risen Christ!

19 / Pray the Model Prayer

Some time ago, the prayer and support group to which I belong studied and prayed the Lord's Prayer together. It was a moving, enriching experience of several weeks. I want to share with you a plan for praying through this matchless prayer found in Matt. 6:9-13. With pencil and journal nearby, you may want to work through the study in one session. More than likely, however, you will want to take whatever time is necessary to hear all that God has for you. Read the selected phrase, meditate on the questions, and be prepared to write as the Lord leads.

Our Father in Heaven.

What do You want to make possible for me this day that neither I nor any other human can make possible? Am I really living and relating to You as if I were Your child? Where does my life display a Kingdom quality? When I pray this prayer in solitude, what does it mean to pray *"our"* Father?

What does "in heaven" mean? In preaching on this passage, Gerhard Ebeling said, "To proclaim God as the God who is near, as Jesus did, is to put an end to the idea of heaven as God's distant dwelling place. . . . It is not that where heaven is, there is God, but rather where God is, there is heaven."[2]

Hallowed Be Your Name.

Let Your name be hallowed, be made holy! Let Your name be hallowed in *my* life! What do You want to make

holy in my life today? How can I facilitate Your name being hallowed in my life? Yesterday, where was Your name
made holy by my life, my presence?

Your Kingdom Come.

Let Your kingdom come, *let* Your kingdom reign!
Whatever it takes in my world for Your kingdom to be es-
tablished, let it be! Where in my life have I been hindering
the coming of Your kingdom? How can Your kingdom
come through me this day? What do I need to do to make
this happen?

Your Will Be Done on Earth As It Is in Heaven.

Let Your will be done! Do I really mean this? Am I
ready for this in my life? What/Where are my Geth-
semanes? Considering the groups of which I am a part
(family, church, work, etc.), how would Your will be done
in those areas? How can I help that to happen? Do I recognize "Your will be done" as a legitimate limit to answered prayer? Am I willing to live it? Am I willing to not
only pray this way but also make this phrase a strong as-
sertion or affirmation in my life?

Give Us Today Our Daily Bread.

What nourishment or help do I need most this day?
What are some ways God has sustained me and my loved
ones in this last year?

What are my deepest *needs* as compared to my most
urgent *wants?* Do I really believe that God is the great Giv-
er? Am I willing to make this a commitment for the whole
of my life? What gifts or resources have already been giv-
en me by God in response to my needs?

Forgive Us Our Debts, As We Also Have Forgiven.

Who do I need most to forgive? Is there something I
can or should do about this today? For what and by whom
do I need most to be forgiven? What do I need to do to

make this happen? What, if any, restitution can or should I make? Is there any way in which I am unwilling to forgive myself?

Lead Us Not into Temptation, but Deliver Us.

Don't allow me to put myself in those dangerous places but deliver me! Help in my weakness! From what do I most need to be protected this day? (Thought, situation, plan, event, dream, person, etc.)

For Yours Is the Kingdom, Power, and Glory.

Where has Your grace most impacted my life? How and where can my life best display and demonstrate Your kingdom, power, and glory?

Take time to pray and live in the Lord's Prayer. Rejoice in the grace and peace of the risen Christ as you do.

20 / Scripture Praying

So often we are outsiders when it comes to reading the Scriptures. We read them from a distance, trying to understand the words and apply them to our daily lives. If we're not careful, we discover we can analyze, strategize, and philosophize the life out of them.

Praying the Scriptures can help. This has been an unknown and neglected method of praying for many of us. Yet it is a contribution to the variety of ways of praying that make this journey such an adventure.

In the depths of each of us there is a desire for a close personal relationship with our Heavenly Father. As we pray the Scriptures, we begin to recognize His loving presence in our days. We begin to think as God thinks, we adopt the mind of Christ as we dwell and pray in the Word.

In the Scriptures we will find the presence of the loving, healing Lord. The Word will speak, and our question will be, "What is God's message for me today?" We will be strengthened, directed, challenged, and led to live a holy life.

There are many ways to enter into Scripture prayer. The joy is trying several until you find the ones you are most comfortable with. From there you can try other methods of praying with the Scriptures.

One way of praying with Scripture is to choose a text, read it meditatively, and let the words apply to us. So often our days are tinged with anxieties and difficulties that tie us into knots. Think of a disturbing situation that happened recently. It may have been something that made you angry with someone. Or it may have been frustration over some situation that did not go right, no matter what you did. Now, read the story of Bartimaeus (Mark 10:46-52).

1. Identify the different kinds of blindness in your life.

2. What causes blindness in your efforts to be with Jesus in your life?

3. Is there any person or situation that consistently blinds you to what you want to see?

4. If Jesus asked you, "What do you want me to do for you?" what would you say?

Now in prayer, see Jesus helping you today, right now, to overcome this blindness. Talk to Him as a friend. Let Him know how you feel. You can be sure that He hears and listens! Tomorrow, try to see everything and everybody with the new sight Jesus has given you in your Scripture prayer.

The Old Testament is rich with material for Scripture praying. Though we need to keep in mind the historical context of the Old Testament passages, many of them can be read as though they were addressed to us today. Take, for example, the beautiful passage in Isa. 43:1-5, which begins: "But now, this is what the Lord says—he who created you, O Jacob, he who formed you, O Israel: 'Fear not, for I have redeemed you.'"

Read the passage through once, then again; but this second time change "Jacob" and "Israel" to your own name. Imagine God speaking directly to you.

1. What do these words mean to you today?

2. The Lord says, "Fear not!" What fears do you have?

3. What are some of your greatest dangers?

4. What, in this passage, does the Lord tell you to do at all times?

God says to you, "You are precious and honored in my sight . . . I love you" (v. 4). How does that make you feel? In prayer, share those feelings with God; tell Him honestly. Let this psalm guide this portion of your prayer time with your Lord.

If you find this kind of praying to be a bit difficult at first, do not be discouraged. In our culture, it is not easy to learn to be quiet and listen to the voice of God in Scripture. The exciting news is that we can *learn* to listen with regular use of Scripture praying. May it be so for you!

21 / What's in a Name?

"In Jesus' name. Amen." I don't know when I was taught to conclude my prayers with that phrase (or one similar), but it was a long time ago! It seemed that a prayer was not *really* a prayer if it did not end "in Jesus' name." I would wonder from time to time about folks who forgot the phrase. Were their prayers nullified?

Some seem to really pray "in Jesus' name" with emphasis and emotion, others as if it is an afterthought and tack it on for safety's sake. There are others who believe the phrase has power of its own, so much so that by its use,

God is cornered into giving whatsoever has been requested! Yet, in Acts 19:13-16, the use of the name of Jesus in casting out demons was not sufficient at all. In fact, it ended in a thorough drubbing by the demon-possessed man!

There seem to be many ideas about what it means to pray in the name of Jesus. Recently, an impromptu poll was taken of a class of students preparing for the ministry. The question was asked, "Why do we pray in Jesus' name?" There were approximately eight different written responses in the group of 35 to 40, ranging from, "Because Jesus is our Mediator and Intercessor" to "I don't know." In between were such answers as "The Bible tells us to," "There is no other name to pray in," and "It provides spiritual power."

In an interesting discussion in *Praying with Power*, Lloyd Ogilvie argues that the name given Jesus that is "above every name" (Phil. 2:9) is really the name for God or Yahweh. It couldn't be Jesus, for there were many by that name before and after the ministry of our Lord. It couldn't be Christ, for that means putting the Messiah above God. It is Jesus, whose name is Yahweh; it is "God with us." Ogilvie concludes his argument by declaring, "Therefore, Jesus' name is Yahweh. That's what is really meant by the words 'in Jesus' name' or more accurately, 'In the name given to Jesus, a name above every name, Yahweh.' *The God who makes things happen is with us and in us to make them continue to happen*" (italics added).[3] In other words, the God of the universe, the Lord, revealed in Christ Jesus, is behind that phrase!

It seems to me that there are several implications to praying in the name of Jesus. At the very least, it means that I pray as a representative of the Lord, Jesus Christ. When I use His name, it is as His ambassador, with all rights, privileges, and powers pertaining thereunto! His representative! It seems fairly clear that it means I am a true disciple, involved in Kingdom business, and abiding in Him. If not, then can I truly represent Him and use His name?

Further, it would seem to mean that to pray in the name of Jesus would be to pray in line with all that His life means. The plumb line of my praying is to be "seek[ing] first the kingdom of God" (Matt. 6:33, KJV). Anything out of line with that simply will not be answered. Nothing that goes against His life, death, resurrection, and return through the Holy Spirit will be honored. In the Bible, the name carried the character of the person. The person was contained in the name. As the Scriptures become more and more the bone, sinew, and muscle of our lives, the more He can lead us to pray in harmony with His character and life.

One more thought: praying in the name of Jesus is to seek promised supernatural power for accomplishing His will. As He guides us in prayer, we ask for the power, through His name, to accomplish His ministry in our world.

Praying in His name will no longer be just habit for me. Ogilvie sums it up well when he says, "We are not meant to use prayer as a desire to get help to do our plan, but power to attempt His plans for us. What in your life could be done only through a supernatural intervention by the living Lord in you? Pray for that!"[4] And, let me add, pray it "in Jesus' name"!

VI

Intercessory Prayer

*At the heart of all prayer, and
certainly intercession, is our willingness to
be at God's disposal, to be available
for any action to which He calls us.*

MAXIE DUNNAM

22 / The Prayer of Intercession

The question haunts me still! In some ways I wish I had not read it. Maxie Dunnam asked it, and I can't get away from it. It's a "what if" question. "What if there were some things God either cannot or will not do until people pray?"[1]

To be honest with you, I'm writing about this subject because I need it. I can only remember a few times when I have been "called" to intercessory prayer in my life—at least in the way I am coming to understand it. Intercessors do pray, but not all of us who pray are intercessors in the true sense of the word—even when we are praying for other people.

For one thing, I am coming to believe that it is God who calls and draws us to intercession. It is through His Holy Spirit that He teaches us what to pray on behalf of others. Lloyd Ogilvie puts it this way: "When He is ready to give reconciliation, salvation, healing, strength, guidance, or the resolution of a seemingly unsolvable problem, He enlists us into partnership for the accomplishment of His will."[2] I am not pleading for God to change His mind; I have come into His presence to find out what it is He wants to do and then to agree with Him and cooperate with Him in the completion of His will.

My second belief about intercession is that it is likely to involve us in action or service beyond prayer. If I think that being an intercessor is a way to stay on the sidelines and be safe, then I had better take another look at the Cross! The Son, who continues to make intercession for us (Heb. 7:25), was *totally* involved! If intercessory prayer is "God putting His burdens on our hearts," as Ogilvie says,[3] then the intercessor not only agrees to pray but also is willing to become a part of the answer. And *that* may be no small challenge!

When we encounter God and discover His will and

plan, we should not stand in shocked surprise when He calls us to give practical assistance to those for whom we have been praying! Kenneth Leech puts it boldly: "Intercession means literally to stand between, to become involved in the conflict."[4]

A third belief is that even though it is God who calls me to it, I can purposely open myself to the ministry of intercessory prayer. I need not sit around waiting for God to speak from heaven. Start with a list. What significant others come to mind who are in need? What about my spouse, children, other family members, friends?

As I come before the Lord, He will be faithful to lead me to those for whom I should intercede. Could it be true that after being converted, our most important ministry is to pray for others? Jesus certainly connected love with prayer when He said, "But I tell you: Love your enemies and pray for those who persecute you, that you may be sons of your Father in heaven" (Matt. 5:44-45).

Prayer is never an excuse for not helping others; but when the circumstances are beyond us, one thing we can do is pray. In fact, it may be the most loving thing we can do.

A nagging question about intercessory prayer remains. Can my prayers for another person really make a difference? Though a good question, maybe it misses the point of intercessory prayer as we have been discussing it. Ogilvie helps me when he says, "The real question is: Can God implant in our minds the maximum expression of His will for another person? Can we cooperate with Him in the accomplishment of His will by praying for him or her? Yes!"

If cooperation is the key, then does that mean that my freedom is minimized? Does it mean that I am just an inert channel through which God works if and when He takes a notion? W. Bingham Hunter, in his book *The God Who Hears*, cites an illustration by T. C. Hammond that may be helpful. A mother cat transports her kittens by grabbing them by the nape of the neck. They go where she goes, whether they like it or not. A baby monkey travels with its mother also, but by clinging to her neck or back. "The mother monkey does the work, but the young one consciously clings. The little monkey goes where the mother goes because it wants to, and this is what happens when Christians pray according to God's will. What God wants, we want; and we seek to pray according to His will."[5]

Back to the original question: "What if there were some things God either cannot or will not do until people pray?" What if, indeed!

23 / The Call to Intercession

"A Christian fellowship lives and exists by the intercession of its members for one another, or it collapses."[6] The more I meditate on that statement by Dietrich Bonhoeffer, the more the call to intercession grips my mind and heart.

Such a declaration raises all sorts of questions. Can intercessory prayer be *that* important? What place does it occupy in the mosaic of my life of prayer? Why is it so hard, and does it really matter anyway? What *is* intercession?

Let's consider the last question first. Some writers suggest that it "is asking God to grant something for another person."[7] Such a definition is headed in the right direction, but I believe there is more to intercession than that. Kenneth Leech says, "Intercessory prayer is not a technique for changing God's mind, but it is a releasing of God's power through placing ourselves in a relationship of cooperation with God."[8] He is speaking here of intentionality, action, and commitment.

In the judgment of Gordon MacDonald, "Intercession usually means prayer on behalf of others. It is the greatest single ministry, in my opinion, that the Christian is privileged to have. And perhaps the most difficult . . . Intercession literally means to stand between two parties and plead the case of one to the other."[9] Here again, the definition points to participation in an activity of cosmic importance.

Henri Nouwen describes intercessory prayer from a more imaginative and contemplative viewpoint when, speaking of the interior life, he says: "To pray for others means to offer others a hospitable place where I can really listen to their needs and pains. Compassion, therefore, calls for a self-scrutiny that can lead to inner gentleness." He goes on to say, "If I could have a gentle 'interiority'—a heart of flesh and not of stone, a room with some spots on which one might walk barefooted—then God and my fellow humans could meet each other there. Then the center of my heart can become the place where God can hear the prayer for my neighbors and embrace them with His love."[10]

All of this is to say that the call to intercession is more than saying (as I have done so many times!), "I'll be praying for you."

Sometime during nearly every prayer retreat or prayer seminar I talk about my journal, which includes my prayer journal. The question usually arises, "What is the difference between *supplication* and *intercession?*" From my perspective, *supplication* is the broader term and includes all my requests of God. *Intercession* has to do with beseeching God on behalf of others and can include the range from family to the world. Therefore, in my journal I have a "prayer list" and an "intercession list."

To get started, in a place of quiet, with some time to spend, try the following exercise. Slowly, meditatively read Eph. 3:14-21 and Col. 1:9-12. Take time to let the Word speak to you; listen to what it is saying. Then, on a sheet of paper, spontaneously list the first six to eight names of persons who come to your mind. List no more than eight, but six will be enough.

In silence, look over your list. Think about each name

individually. What would you like God to do for them? Within the knowledge you have, what are their deepest concerns? Is there illness, depression, anxiety? Is there a battle with loneliness, a moral problem or grief? Has there been a heavy loss of some kind? What are their struggles? In a word or two, indicate these needs to the right of each name. Now let this list be the beginning of your ministry of intercessory prayer and a great adventure with God.

24 / How to Pray for Other People

The Bible coaches us to fill up a big chunk of our prayer time with the names of others. In Gen. 18:23-33, for example, Abraham pleads to God about sparing Sodom. Is there any more stirring intercession than Moses entreating God to spare His anger against Israel (Exod. 32:11-13, 31-32)?

In the New Testament, the Gospels show Jesus' interceding for the disciples. Further, John lets us know that Jesus prayed for those who were to come after them, including you and me! He prayed: "My prayer is not for them alone, I pray also for those who will believe in me through their message, that all of them may be one, Father, just as you are in me and I am in you" (John 17:20-21). Not only so, but in Hebrews we read: "Therefore he is able to save completely those who come to God through him, because he always lives to intercede for them" (7:25).

The priority of prayer shows up again when the Early Church attacked the problem of food distribution. "Choose seven men from among you who are known to be full of the Spirit and wisdom. We will turn this responsibility over to them and will give our attention to prayer and the ministry of the word" (Acts 6:3-4). Surely this prayer program included intercession for the lost, particularly the "lost sheep of Israel." How quickly those spiritual ancestors of ours learned that a lot of good activities can change prayer to a mere "spare time" exercise.

Believing in the priority of intercession, how do I go about it? Acceptable methods for intercessory prayer may outnumber hamburger recipes. That's what makes this prayer journey so creative and dynamic. Let me share just three "recipes" for praying for others. I hope they release you to begin an intercessory prayer ministry that bears the distinctive gifts of your own personality.

Leslie D. Weatherhead, in an older but creative work, uses a list numbered 1 to 31 with space for four names per number. On the day of the month you are praying, you can concentrate on the four names by that number. Of course there will be conditions and situations that will change the format, but at least it provides an organized approach when needed.[11]

Expanding on the list idea, Donald Bloesch relates the story of the veteran missionary to China, Charles Whiston, who had a prayer list of over 2,000 names! Each name was kept on a 3" x 5" card. Every day, during his prayer time, Whiston went through the cards and by the end of the week had prayed for every name.[12]

Imagination is a powerful tool in intercessory prayer. I like Maxie Dunnam's method. This approach centers around having a three-way conversation with the person praying, the person for whom we are praying, and Jesus. Imagine the three of you in some comfortable location that is easy for you to see in your mind's eye. It could be around the fireplace, walking through a park, or at the dinner table.

Then simply create a conversation with Jesus about the person for whom you are praying as though that person were actually present. This method works well for me when I am praying not only for those who are known and near but also for persons far away and less well known to me.

Why not try this method for a week? You can practice it almost anywhere, while busy around the home or on your way to work. Choose someone with whom you have had a difficult relationship, or someone for whom you are concerned. Each day imagine this three-way conversation with Jesus and see what happens.[13]

As you have been thinking and praying these past few weeks, has God been calling you to intercession? If you were to picture yourself as developing such a ministry, what would your prayer life look like? How would it be different?

Would you have any prayer partners? Would you spend more effort in prayer on the names and needs of others than on your own bruises and blessings? What if Christians everywhere made real intercession a way of life?

25 / The Prayer for Healing

What a joy! To know that the Church is called not only to preach and teach but to heal as well. In a world that seems bent on going to pieces, Jesus' followers offer a message of hope, reconciliation, and wholeness. In prayer, we can intercede for the desperate needs of those whom God loves and desires to see whole.

Over the years, a maze of conflicting opinions about prayer for healing have kept me hesitant and off-balance. I've come, however, to some understanding about this liberating ministry Jesus has given to the Church.

For me, healing prayer begins with the belief that God's ultimate will is for wholeness in mind, body, and spirit. A study of the word used for "save" in the New Testament (James 5:15, KJV, for example) means "salvation" and "wholeness." The person was seen holistically; they were to find healing for the whole person, not just the spirit. It was not until later in history that concern for the salvation of the spirit overshadowed the need for physical and emotional wholeness.

As I study the life and ministry of Jesus, I am deeply impressed with His concern for hurting persons. The lame walked, the blind were made to see, the emotionally shattered were given peace—and the dead were brought to life! The God who loves me does not delight in my sufferings! He longs to see me made whole. However, that wholeness may not come according to my calculations, and that brings me to my second faith statement.

What happens or does not happen when I pray for healing is entirely in the hands of a sovereign God. Let me not fall into the trap of thinking that by praying according to a certain formula, saying precise words, demanding God to act, or relying on "enough faith," I can manipulate or force Him to respond according to my wishes. When I pray for healing, I do it in the answer to His gracious invitation to do so. I rest in the sovereign, loving will of God for my life and for those for whom I pray. He is in charge—and that's OK.

After all, to be healed may not be what we *really* want! It is more than just interesting that on several occasions Jesus did not heal until He had asked the question, in one form or another, "What do you want Me to do for you?" In essence, I believe He was asking, "Do you *really* want to be healed?" It's a good question. For some of us, if we were to find ourselves without our "malady," we would be lonely! What would we talk about? What would take up our time? This leads me to my third belief about healing prayer.

Healing calls us to humility, commitment, and service. When healed, we may find ourselves called back into our world with more responsibility than ever before. At the very least, it will be cause for humble praise and sincere commitment to doing what we can to alleviate the suffering around us. We finally come to the realization that physical healing here on earth is never permanent. Perfect healing will come only when we enter into His presence for eternity. This helps me keep my own healing and the healing of those for whom I have prayed in proper perspective. It is only one part of the ministry to which we are called, be it a very *significant* part.

Finally, I believe healing prayer is most accurately perceived when it is seen as an ongoing, natural ministry of the whole Church, the Body of Christ. Rather than a special activity with the temptation of drawing attention to certain individuals, it ought to be part and parcel of the array of ministries offered by the Christian community for the reconciling and healing of humankind.

In 1968 our daughter was diagnosed with a problem that called for surgery. The day before we were to drop by the doctor's office for a final checkup, our pastor, Earl Lee, called and said he felt impressed to come by our home to pray and anoint Dana with oil. This did not seem unusual to us because one Sunday morning a month was set aside for healing prayer at the altar before services began. Also, we knew that anyone could ask for prayer for healing at the close of almost any service, and many did so.

Pastor Lee came by, we knelt by the living room coffee table, and our daughter was prayed for and anointed.

The next day we went to the doctor's office before going to the hospital. After the examination, the doctor stepped back and said, "I don't know what has happened, but there is no need for surgery. I'll go ahead and cancel the appointment." We rejoiced in God's loving action, but as I look back, there was no overwhelming surprise. It was a natural part of the environment of a loving, praying, healing community.

Our greatest trap in praying for healing is concern over the results. Lloyd Ogilvie, in *Praying with Power,* says, "Once we get free of judging the Lord for the results of our prayers we are liberated to pray boldly and leave the outcome to Him . . . An awesome trust has been given to us to pray for healing. The power to do that is the Lord's and not ours. What is our responsibility is to keep the power lines open."[14]

VII

Fundamentals of Prayer

*God has ordained the Disciplines of the
spiritual life as the means by which
we are placed where He can bless us.*

RICHARD FOSTER

26 / Fundamentals for a Life of Prayer

Recently, a seemingly simple question has captured my attention. "What are the elements necessary to a life of prayer?" In other words, what's the bottom line to an effective prayer journey with God? The question assumes a saving relationship with the Lord Jesus Christ. But beyond that, what cannot be left out if one is serious about developing prayerful communication with God? Maybe the query is not so simple after all!

I don't think I have all the answers, but let me share some of the clues that have been dawning on me. You can improve on these ideas, but let's at least think together on this vital issue.

The most crucial element to a worthwhile prayer life is *intentionality*. Without intention, prayer will not happen, except in moments of life's emergencies. We are all acquainted with "foxhole" prayers of one kind or another. When life comes crashing in, the human spirit instinctively calls out to its Creator. But that is not the kind of praying we are giving attention to in this book. A life of prayer happens only when we *intend* to pray.

The prayer life of Jesus is always instructive. In Mark 1:35 we read, "Very early in the morning, while it was still dark, Jesus got up, left the house and went off to a solitary place, where he prayed." No happenstance praying here. You can feel the purposeful, deliberate choice He has made to pray.

The trouble with *intentionality* is that it sounds so much like *commitment* or *discipline,* and we don't like those words. We don't want them to apply to the life lived in the "freedom of the Spirit," but they do! If I am going to develop a mature life of prayer, then I will *intend* to do it. I will make the commitment necessary! If I do not begin here, then I should not be too surprised if I end up with an impotent prayer life.

It's interesting—I have no trouble with this concept when it comes to anything else worthwhile in life. If I dream of becoming an artist, musician, teacher, minister, mechanic, or whatever—without intentionality, without commitment, it will never happen.

Another vital element to an ongoing prayer life is *consistency*. I am not suggesting here a regulated timetable that others ought to follow. The issue is pattern. When viewed over a given length of time, is prayer evident in any consistent manner? The design may have holes and gaps here and there, but a visible pattern should appear.

Again, Jesus sets the paradigm. Not only did He pray early in the morning, but He prayed at other times too. "After leaving them, he went up on a mountainside to pray. When evening came, the boat was in the middle of the lake, and he was alone on land" (Mark 6:46-47). "One of those days Jesus went out to a mountainside to pray, and spent the night praying to God" (Luke 6:12). "But Jesus often withdrew to lonely places and prayed" (5:16).

Prayer was such a consistent occurrence in His life that it was evident to anyone who knew Him at all. His life of prayer invited the disciples to ask Him to teach them how to pray. His intentionality and consistency were compelling! There was a rhythm of prayer to His life and ministry. It was into the crowds to heal and restore, getting alone to pray, back to ministry with the multitudes, withdrawing to be with the Father.

Whereas intentionality speaks of commitment, consistency points to obedience. Intentionality is only "good intentions" without the follow-through of consistent obedience. Do I respond to Jesus' call to prayer with any pattern at all?

I have come to realize that those who seem to pray so effortlessly and constantly have built their prayer sojourns by intention and consistency. They made a commitment and were obedient. What I am privileged to witness is the overflow!

27 / More Fundamentals for a Life of Prayer

We have proposed that where intentionality spoke of commitment, consistency suggested obedience and discipline. It is not surprising that anything worthwhile in life begins with these two building blocks. It is no less true in developing a life characterized by the pattern of prayer.

A third fundamental to effective prayer is *expectancy*. Praying is not just another duty or obligation in the list of Christian "oughts." We do not pray in order to qualify as a good Christian. Rather, we come to the Father with expectancy. It speaks of faith and of hope. What then should I *expect* (have faith for) when I pray?

First, I can expect a Presence. I can have faith that when I come to the secret place, my Heavenly Father will be there to meet me. He *wants* to be with me; He wants me to know Him. The whole of John 17, Jesus' high-priestly prayer, demonstrates an acute awareness of the presence of the Heavenly Father. No empty, dutiful praying here; there is communication and communion!

Second, I can expect a hearing. Part of the drawing and attraction to prayer is the belief that I *will* be heard! It is the living, personal, hearing God who waits for me to come into His presence. Isaiah declares, "O people of Zion, who live in Jerusalem, you will weep no more. How gracious he will be when you cry for help! As soon as he hears, he will answer you" (30:19). The Psalmist assures us, "The Lord will hear when I call to him" (4:3).

Expectancy, or *prayer in faith,* is not the same as *faith in prayer.* Maxie Dunnam puts it this way:

> Certainly *faith in prayer* may be presumptuous and clamorous, presenting ultimatums to God and demanding his acquiescence. But *prayer in faith* is different. It may ask and keep on asking. Indeed it may be

clamorous. But all that the asking and pleading is, is entire submission to the will of God. Our faith is not in prayer, but in God. In prayer we may plead passionately for our needs, but our faith is in God; thus we can close our petitions as Jesus did, "Thy will be done."[1]

Which brings me to the fourth and final essential element in a life of prayer, that of *humility*. Humility speaks of submission and of rest. As Dunnam has suggested, if your faith is in prayer (which usually means obvious, positive answers), then we may be in trouble. However, to pray in faith (or expectancy) is to be willing to acknowledge the sovereignty of God and His right to answer my prayer in any way He deems best for me. In fact, that is exactly where my faith resides, that in all things God is working for the good of those who love Him (Rom. 8:28).

Humility is to realize that there is no higher prayer (and probably none more difficult) than "Thy will be done." It is significant to me that at the end of His ministry, Jesus, the Son of God, ended His prayer in Gethsemane with such a declaration (Matt. 26:42).

We need to acknowledge that praying "Thy will be done" can be approached in at least two ways. One is to see it as fatalistic and hopeless. It is to decide that the situation is so far gone that I pray in a spirit of resignation. This can lead to despair, discouragement, and depression.

The other approach is to pray out of faith and deep hope in the One who died and lives again! This is the God who paid the ultimate price for our redemption and who loves us beyond our comprehension. He *wills* the very best for us and sees to it that His will is carried out! I can pray in true submission and rest, "Nevertheless, Thy will be done"!

What an honor it is to address the holy God, to come into His presence with boldness. To think that He would stoop to listen and hear me, that is good enough. How and when He answers matters little in the light of His willingness to shower me with His grace and live His life through me. What more could I ask?

28 / How Can You Pray for One Hour? (Part 1)

Once again I had gone through the motions. With the sincerest of motives I intended to make prayer a priority in my life, a meaningful segment of my daily walk. Yet, when I was done, I wasn't at all sure just what it was that I prayed about. I would start off well, then seem to drift to the Amen.

Has that ever happened to you? Have you ever wondered what it was you were supposed to pray about during your quiet time with Him? Three minutes seems like a manageable possibility, but 30 minutes is another matter! And some folks advocate an hour! What do you do for an hour?

Finally, it dawned on me that in any activity of life a disciplined way of doing things is the only way to success. To be good at tennis or painting takes dedication to some routine or method. Creativity and genius may find their way into the process, but it will be *because* of a consistent method, not *in spite* of it.

So it is with prayer. Not only does a consistent approach lead to more fulfilling prayer times, but it keeps me balanced in my approach to God. Without some guideline or pattern, it is too easy for me to concentrate in just one or two pet areas.

There are many ways to organize our prayer times. One way of organizing prayer stands out for its historical and biblical significance and for its simplicity. It is the familiar *ACTS* method. Most approaches of which I am aware include these four aspects in one way or another.

The *A* stands for adoration, the *C* for confession, the letter *T* for thanksgiving, and *S* signifies supplication. A simple, easily remembered way to pray in a biblical and balanced manner. I need that!

Adoration. Something happens when I begin my time with God in adoration, worship, and praise. For so many years I rushed into His presence with one thing on my mind, *my* needs and *my* requests. I do not remember being taught *how* to praise and adore our Heavenly Father with purpose and clarity of thought. How do I worship Him?

Begin by taking time to reflect on who He is, His majesty, power, and all-knowing presence. To contemplate the many facets of His character is to know what it means to "give worth" to God, or in other words, to worship.

We might spend time in the Psalms. One writer suggests reading Psalms 95 through 108, one each day for two weeks.[2] Another author finds Psalms 8, 19, 23, 46, 95, and 100 especially helpful.[3] By searching the Psalms yourself, you may find something excitingly different, and just right for you!

The most helpful idea I have used was shared by a dear friend. It is to adore the Lord by working my way through the alphabet. Sometimes I use nouns, and at other times they turn out to be adjectives; it just depends. For example, I might begin by saying, "Lord, today I adore You, for You are *a*lmighty and yet my *A*dvocate. You are *b*oundless love and my *b*lessed Redeemer. . . ." I think you get the idea. By keeping a journal, I can go back each day, noting where I left off, and also expand my "adoration vocabulary."

Confession. This could be one of the most neglected areas in our private prayer lives today. One aspect of confession is "profession." It is professing that Jesus Christ is truly God. In the book *Praying,* Bobb Biehl and James Hagelganz put it this way:

> The starting point of confession—true confession—
> is to profess Jesus to be God. This confession cannot be

mere words. It must be the result of a deep conviction that He is our only source of eternal hope and salvation. At the heart of this kind of confession is the idea that we cannot make it on our own. As humans we can do absolutely nothing to save our own souls. We are entirely and absolutely dependent on Him.[4]

I need to declare this truth time and again.

Another aspect of confession is agreeing with God concerning our condition. It is the willingness to forgive unconditionally and to seek to be forgiven, whenever such needs are pointed out by His Spirit. Our Wesleyan theological heritage does not declare that it is *impossible* to sin, but that it is *possible not* to sin! There is a big difference. My opinion is, if somehow we could learn to live and pray confessionally in the spirit of 1 John 1:6—2:2, it would go a long way to setting the Holy Spirit free in our midst.

Today, why not at least attempt to develop a consistent pattern of adoration and confession as you begin your prayer time? Try working your way through the alphabet in adoration. Then write out a prayer of confession, including both elements we have discussed here. Adapt the ideas in any way that suits your own approach. How exciting it is to build a powerful prayer life!

29 / How Can You Pray for One Hour? (Part 2)

Having discussed Adoration and Confession in the ACTS method of prayer, we now turn our attention to Thanksgiving and Supplication.

Thanksgiving. After I have worshiped and adored the Lord as a beginning to my prayer time and have moved on to true confession, thanksgiving becomes a natural and orderly response. The Scriptures abound with references to thanks and thanksgiving. It is to become a way of life in the maturing Christian. One of the most powerful references is found in 1 Thess. 5:16-18: "Be joyful always; pray continually; give thanks in all circumstances, for this is God's will for you in Christ Jesus."

Can we talk? Before going further, I want to comment on "give thanks in all circumstances." It says *in,* not *for.* I think there is a significant difference. I am not to try to thank God *for* everything that happens to me, but *in* every situation I can be thankful that God is acting on my behalf; I am not left alone. It is difficult for me to thank God for the evil that impacts my life, the tragedies, suffering, and evil brought on by others. But I *can* express thanks to the Creator God, who brings order out of chaos, who works for my good in the midst of the worst, and who demonstrated this love through the Cross and the Resurrection!

There are many things for which we can thank our Heavenly Father. We can thank Him for who He is and what He has done, for answers to prayer, for spiritual and material blessings, and for what He is doing in the lives of others. As we begin to learn how to live a life of thanksgiving, the possibilities become endless.

Try making a list of items for which you are thankful in your prayer journal. Let it be a reference point when praying. Let the list build itself as you come back to it day after day, adding to it as the Lord brings new entries to mind.

Supplication. This category can include such items as petition and intercession. It is asking God for our needs. For so long I moved to petition way too early in my prayer time. How much more fulfilling it is now to spend time in adoration, confession, and thanksgiving, and *then* move to supplication.

Lest we feel guilty about praying for *our* needs, consider the following:

"Ask and it will be given to you; seek and you will find; knock and the door will be opened to you. For everyone who asks receives; he who seeks finds; and to him who knocks, the door will be opened" (Matt. 7:7-8).

"Do not be anxious about anything, but in everything, by prayer and petition, with thanksgiving, present your requests to God" (Phil. 4:6).

"You do not have, because you do not ask God" (James 4:2).

God wants us to ask Him to help us. It is a way of demonstrating our total dependence on Him. There is nothing too big for Him to handle, and nothing too small for Him to care about. Ps. 37:4 is a promise worth memorizing: "Delight yourself in the Lord and he will give you the desires of your heart."

In thinking about asking God for what I need, a poem by Garth and Merv Rosell has been an inspiration to me:

I asked for strength that I might achieve;
He made me weak that I might obey.
I asked for health that I might do greater things:
I was given grace that I might do better things.
I asked for riches that I might be happy;
I was given poverty that I might be wise.
I asked for power that I might have the praise of men;
I was given weakness that I might feel the need of God.
I asked for all things that I might enjoy life;
I was given life that I might enjoy all things.
I received nothing that I asked for, all that I hoped for;
My prayer was answered.[5]

30 / Try a Prayer Journal

It seems that not a day goes by but that I forget something! If it is the same for you, then you understand the feeling. There are other times when I remember very well moments in the past that remain vibrant and alive with sights, sounds, and emotions still as powerful as when they were first experienced.

Memory is a powerful thing. Henri Nouwen, in his book *The Living Reminder*, suggests four key factors about memory.

First, many of our human emotions are tied to our memory. Guilt, gratitude, regret, and other emotions are significantly affected by the way we have incorporated past events into our world.

Second, it is the strategy of the enemy to cut us off from the memory of God. As we drift in our relationship with Him, our frenetic activities speak more and more of our growing disorientation and dimming commitment.

Third, "good memories offer good guidance." In the midst of distress comes hope buoyed by a good memory. In the darkness, we can believe in the light, because we have seen the light before.

And fourth, for Israel, remembering was more than just looking back. To remember an event was to bring it into the present, to *live* it again. When sharing the Last Supper with His disciples, Jesus said, "Do this in remembrance of me" (1 Cor. 11:24). The idea of *living* and *experiencing* the memory adds deeper meaning to this most central sacrament.[6]

This reflection on the power of memory helps enrich my concept of a prayer journal.

A prayer journal or notebook can be a source of spiritual development in several ways. It can bring order out of chaos to our prayer lives. How often I have gone for days, forgetting to pray for a situation or person. How much more effective to come to prayer with a journal, listing my growing concerns there on the page where they are easily remembered. It can be a source of a developing life-style of thanksgiving. As you review what God has done in the past, praise and gratitude become a natural response to a loving God. It is reported that there are over 50,000 specific answers to prayer recorded in George Mueller's prayer notebook, *God's Dealings with George Mueller.*

A prayer journal helps us see our growing maturity. We are not always aware of what is going on in the moment. On our kitchen wall there are 10 penciled hash marks, marking the periodic growth of our son. When in doubt about his growth over the past year, the marks proved it—and always to his delight!

Finally, a prayer notebook helps us stay in touch with reality and humility. When we want to take credit for some accomplishment, a review of our journal helps us see that it was really an answer to prayer and God's doing, not ours. *He* deserves the praise and the glory.

What goes into a prayer notebook? There are many ways to do it. Simplicity is a key, and the point is to start—today! Begin with what comes naturally to you. It may be as simple as a single sheet of paper with a list of prayer requests showing the date the request was entered and the date it was answered. Another suggestion is to transfer an answered request to another sheet titled "Answers to Prayer."

As the journal becomes a normal practice, you may want to add other sections. Biehl and Hagelganz, in their little book, *Praying*, suggest divisions such as: Praise, Confession, Thanksgiving, Petition, and Intercession.[7] When using multiple sections, a three-ring binder will facilitate adding, removing, and changing pages and sections.

What might your prayer life be like if you tried a prayer list, journal, or notebook for 30 days? I cannot tell you the joy I have found in reviewing my notebook at each prayer time, giving praise and thanksgiving for who God is and rejoicing in the evidence of answered prayer in my life. They are powerful memories because they have been captured on paper rather than lost in forgetfulness.

Don't be immobilized by indecision; just start. Remember, you *can't* do it wrong!

31 / Responses to a Prayer Journal

We have talked about the rewards of keeping a prayer journal. I have received several inspiring letters from those who have found the prayer journal fruitful. With their permission, I want to share a couple of them with you.

Denise writes:

> It was your article in the *Herald* that has initiated this letter! In October, God sent me a very special friend. On January 9, we were sharing together, and she began to describe the frustration of her double life. There were some things that she needed to take care of and asked me to pray for her. She had said she'd call when she was through.
>
> I waited all afternoon and evening with no phone call. In the night God woke me and revealed my inadequate prayer life. I fought with Him until 6 A.M.— when I finally submitted and began to learn to pray. For the next 30 hours—through prayer and reading "The Power of Prayer"—I began a "brand-new" walk with the Lord. This was much different than anything I've ever experienced.
>
> This is where your article comes in! To encourage my friend, she and I began meeting at 6:45 A.M. for prayer each day before school. What an incredible difference that began to make in us as individuals, as well as teachers! She shared with me about a prayer journal—something she had done in college. I had *never* been *that* committed to prayer before and had never done anything like that. So, we agreed together to start one, to help keep us "on track." What a tremendous blessing that has become! It really almost calls for me to keep in tune with God!
>
> Let me tell you what has happened now in the last two months. My friend has joined our church, teaches our young adults class, and has been instrumental in leading at least three individuals back to

God! We still have our prayer time *every* morning, along with four or five other teachers. We've had so many miraculous answers to prayer—I couldn't begin to name them. I'm amazed that I lived 17 years with the Lord and *never* caught a glimpse of what "real" prayer could do. So, I said all this to say thanks for your article!

Another inspiring letter came from Sharon. She writes:

A few weeks ago I read your article on trying a prayer journal. During seminary I remember writing down so many answers to prayer. Over the years, parenthood, work, and the duties of a pastor's wife crowded out that time to write. Eight weeks ago, on a Sunday night, I lay in bed not able to sleep, worrying about how we would pay $600 we owed in taxes. I had tried to be frugal and save, but invariably the car would need fixing, or some other calamity would occur, and there was nothing left over. I began pitying my circumstances as the wife of a home mission church pastor, bemoaning our plight to God. Suddenly, a firm inner voice spoke: "I own the cattle on a thousand hills! What do you need? Ask Me! Have I ever failed you?"

At first I shot back, "You own the cattle on a thousand hills, but how are You going to bring me $600?"

"REMEMBER," God said.

And as I lay there, the miracles of answered prayer I had recorded those months in seminary came back to mind—answers long forgotten and probably never remembered except for having been written and reread in my journal. I wept, asked forgiveness, and meditated on the words of the hymn "God Will Take Care of You," then fell soundly to sleep.

The next morning while substitute teaching, a note was brought in asking me to come to the principal's office as soon as possible. The principal said one of the teachers had suddenly gone in for emergency

surgery. Could I begin a long-term assignment immediately? It paid extra, over and above my substitute's
normal pay. In fact (and she paused to look it up),
$600 extra! Could I use the money?

I sat stunned. Speechless. I could hardly find my
voice to answer. In less than 18 hours my prayer had
been answered.

Today, eight weeks later, I was again substituting,
my long-term assignment over. On a break, I pulled
out the *Herald* and began looking through it. I reread
your article on a prayer journal. Suddenly, I realized I
had never even written down the miracle that had so
recently occurred. I took out paper and with an over-
flowing heart, finished my testimony to God's abun-
dant grace, to add to my journal of miracles.

God is always on the throne, yet how often we
forget. As you said, "It is the strategy of the enemy to
cut us off from the memory of God," and "Good memories offer good guidance."

Notes

Section I: Prayer of the Heart

1. E. Stanley Jones, *Mastery* (New York: Abingdon, 1955), 288.

2. Oswald Chambers, *My Utmost for His Highest* (New York: Dodd, Mead, and Co., 1935), 219.

3. James C. Fenhagen, *More than Wanderers* (Minneapolis: Seabury Press, 1978), 29.

4. W. Bingham Hunter, *The God Who Hears* (Downers Grove, Ill.: InterVarsity Press, 1986), 116.

5. Chambers, *My Utmost for His Highest,* 147.

6. David Hubbard, *Practice of Prayer* (Downers Grove, Ill.: InterVarsity Press, 1972), 67.

7. Henri Nouwen, *The Way of the Heart* (New York: Seabury Press, 1981), 79.

8. Maxie Dunnam, *The Workbook of Living Prayer* (Nashville: Upper Room, 1974), 100.

9. Wes Tracy, editorial in the *Herald of Holiness,* January 1991.

10. Richard Foster, *Celebration of Discipline* (San Francisco: Harper and Row, 1978), 14, italics added.

11. Susan Muto, *Pathways of Spiritual Living* (Petersham, Mass.: St. Bede's Publications, 1974), 83.

12. Foster, *Celebration of Discipline,* 15.

13. Ibid., 17.

14. Muto, *Pathways of Spiritual Living,* 90-91.

Section II: Obstacles to Prayer

1. Lewis Smedes, *Christianity Today,* Jan. 7, 1983, 26.

2. Chambers, *My Utmost for His Highest,* 241.

3. Woodrow M. Kroll, "The Peril of Prayerlessness," *Fundamentalist Journal* 4 (July—August 1985): 21-22.

4. Gordon MacDonald, *Ordering Your Private World* (Nashville: Thomas Nelson, 1985), 145-50.

5. Kenneth Leech, *True Prayer* (San Francisco: Harper and Row, 1980), 166.

6. Henri Nouwen, "Letting Go of All Things," *Sojourners,* May 1979, 5.

7. Chambers, *My Utmost for His Highest,* 241.

8. Archibald Hart, *Counseling the Depressed* (Dallas: Word Books, 1987), 24 ff.

9. Ted Loder, "The Unclenched Moment," in *Guerrillas of Grace* (San Diego: Lura Media, 1984), 17.

10. Susan Muto, *Meditation in Motion* (Garden City, N.Y.: Image Books, 1986), 103-6.

Section III: The Question of Unanswered Prayer

1. Anthony Bloom, *Beginning to Pray* (London: Darton, Longman, and Todd, 1970), 26-31.

2. Lloyd Ogilvie, *Praying with Power* (Ventura, Calif.: Regal Books, 1983), 88.

3. Ibid., 80.

4. Bill Hybels, *Too Busy Not to Pray* (Downers Grove, Ill.: InterVarsity Press, 1988), 78.

5. Ogilvie, *Praying with Power*, 82.

6. Ibid., 84.

7. Hybels, *Too Busy Not to Pray*, 81.

8. Calvin Miller, *The Table of Inwardness* (Downers Grove, Ill.: InterVarsity Press, 1984), 68.

9. Archibald Hart, *15 Principles for Achieving Happiness* (Dallas: Word Books, 1988), n.p.

Section IV: Silence and Prayer

1. Nouwen, *Way of the Heart*, 47-48.

2. Henri Nouwen, *The Living Reminder* (New York: Seabury Press, 1977), 52.

3. Bob Benson, *Disciplines for the Inner Life* (Waco, Tex.: Word Books, 1985), 35.

4. Nouwen, *Way of the Heart*, 22.

5. Miller, *Table of Inwardness*, 71-72.

6. Wayne Oates, *Nurturing Silence in a Noisy Heart* (Garden City, N.Y.: Doubleday, 1979), 113.

Section V: Praying the Scriptures

1. Leonard E. LeSourd, *Touching the Heart of God* (Old Tappan, N.J.: Chosen Books, 1990), 125.

2. Gerhard Ebeling, *On Prayer* (Philadelphia: Fortress Press, 1966), 50.

3. Ogilvie, *Praying with Power*, 105.

4. Ibid., 107.

Section VI: Intercessory Prayer

1. Maxie Dunnam, *The Workbook of Intercessory Prayer* (Nashville: Upper Room, 1979), 15.

2. Ogilvie, *Praying with Power*, 68.

3. Ibid., 63.

4. Leech, *True Prayer*, 25.

5. Hunter, *The God Who Hears*, 58.

6. Benson, *Disciplines for the Inner Life*, 71.

7. Bobb Biehl and James Hagelganz, *Praying: How to Start and Keep Going* (Sisters, Oreg.: Questar Pub., 1989), 72.

8. Leech, *True Prayer*, 25.

9. MacDonald, *Ordering Your Private World*, 155.

10. Benson, *Disciplines for the Inner Life*, 74.

11. Leslie D. Weatherhead, *A Private House of Prayer* (New York: Abingdon, 1958), 26.

12. Donald G. Bloesch, *The Struggle of Prayer* (San Francisco: Harper and Row, 1980), 89.

13. Dunnam, *Workbook of Intercessory Prayer*, 119-20.

14. Ogilvie, *Praying with Power*, 101-2.

Section VII: Fundamentals of Prayer

1. Dunnam, *Workbook of Intercessory Prayer*, 25.

2. Ogilvie, *Praying with Power*, 26.

3. Hybels, *Too Busy Not to Pray*, 53.

4. Biehl and Hagelganz, *Praying*, 32.

5. Ibid., 69.

6. Nouwen, *Living Reminder*, n.p.

7. Biehl and Hagelganz, *Praying*, 19-71.